W9-DJC-079

Creating 6-Trait Revisers and Editors for Grade 6

Creating 6-Trait Revisers and Editors for Grade 6

30 Revision and Editing Lessons

Vicki Spandel

Writer in Residence, Great Source Education Group

PEARSON

Boston New York San Francisco
Mexico City Montreal Toronto London Madrid Munich Paris
Hong Kong Singapore Tokyo Cape Town Sydney

Thank you to the following individuals for reviewing this book.
Dena Harrison, Mendive Middle School
Patti Taillacq, Marlborough Intermediate Elementary School
Rebecca Zieminski, Marlborough Intermediate Elementary School

Executive Editor: Aurora Martínez Ramos
Editorial Assistant: Kara Kikel
Executive Marketing Manager: Krista Clark
Marketing Manager: Danae April
Production Editor: Janet Domingo
Editorial-Production Service: Kathy Smith
Composition Buyer: Linda Cox
Manufacturing Buyer: Megan Cochran
Interior Design and Composition: Schneck-DePippo Graphics
Cover Administrator: Linda Knowles

For related titles and support materials, visit our online catalog at www.allynbaconmerrill.com.

Copyright © 2009 Pearson Education, Inc.

All rights reserved. No part of the material protected by this copyright notice may be reproduced or utilized in any form or by any means, electronic or mechanical, including photocopying, recording, or by any information storage and retrieval system, without written permission from the copyright owner.

To obtain permission(s) to use material from this work, please submit a written request to Allyn and Bacon, Permissions Department, 501 Boylston Street, Suite 900, Boston, MA 02116, or fax your request to 617-671-2290.

Between the time website information is gathered and then published, it is not unusual for some sites to have closed. Also, the transcription of URLs can result in typographical errors. The publisher would appreciate notification where these errors occur so that they may be corrected in subsequent editions.

ISBN-13: 978-0-205-57061-4   ISBN-10: 0-205-57061-5

Printed in the United States of America
10 9 8 7 6 5 4 3 2 1   Bind-Rite 12 11 10 09 08

**Allyn & Bacon
is an imprint of**

www.allynbaconmerrill.com

Contents

Creating Revisers and Editors

Welcome!

. . . to a series of revision and editing lessons that challenge students to be daring and confident revisers.

These lessons complement and extend instructional ideas found in my book *Creating Writers Through 6-Trait Assessment and Instruction* (for grades 3 through college). In this set of lessons—as suggested in my book—students practice revision and editing skills on text that is *not their own*, and then extend what they have learned by applying those same strategies to their own writing.

Unlike other writing and revising lessons, this set of lessons shows revision *in action*. It allows students to see drafts in process, observe exactly what a thoughtful reviser does, and compare this to their own revision of the very same text. Students work individually, with partners, and in groups, and have multiple chances to experience success.

> **Please note that these lessons are a perfect complement to your own instruction or any materials, such as the *Write Traits Classroom Kits* (by Vicki Spandel and Jeff Hicks), that you may use to teach *ideas, organization, voice, word choice, sentence fluency,* and *conventions*.**

Why do we need to teach revision differently?

Traditionally, we have not really *taught* revision at all. We have only *assigned* it: "Revise this for Monday." Students who do not understand revision or who have not learned specific strategies to apply often wind up writing a longer draft, making it neater, or correcting conventional errors. This is not true revision. Revising is re-seeing, re-thinking text, and making internal changes that affect message, voice, and readability.

The six traits make it possible for us to actually *teach* revision. In order to do so effectively, however, we have to make revision visible. This starts with providing rubrics and checklists that clarify expectations. But this is *not enough*. We must show students what revision looks like, by taking a rough draft and marking it up with arrows, carets, delete symbols, and new text. The lessons in this book:

Extend students' practice. Most students practice revision and editing only on their own work. Because very few of them write and revise every day, such an approach does not offer nearly enough practice to ensure growth in skill and understanding. By working on the text of other writers, students develop skills they can apply to their own work. Not only does their writing improve, but students become significantly more efficient, confident revisers.

Show students what revision looks like. Many teachers are uncomfortable writing with or in front of students, feel they do not have time to write, or are unsure about what modeling looks like, and so they do not attempt it. As a result, most students have never seen what other writers actually *do* when they write or revise. In addition, much of the writing students do is on computer or via text messaging. The revision is either invisible (once a change is made, the history of the draft is gone) or non-existent! In these lessons, the original text remains in place, with changes superimposed so students can track what is happening.

Make revision manageable. As students move into middle grades and beyond, their writing tends to get longer, and the idea of tackling revision on a two-, three-, or five-page document, especially when they must deal with everything at once, overwhelms many of them. With this set of lessons, students work on smaller text, and focus on one problem (or a small handful of problems) at a time. This gives them confidence to take on something bigger.

What if I have never worked with the traits before?

One glance through this book will assure you that these are pick-up-and-go lessons. You will find this revision and editing practice *very* student- and teacher friendly, even if you are new to the traits.

At the same time, I urge you to use these lessons in conjunction with the book *Creating Writers*, Fifth edition (2009, Pearson Education). These lessons are an extension of ideas put forth in that text. The book offers *numerous* additional writing samples instructional strategies to help you to understand:

■ What the six traits are.

■ How they influence written text.

■ How to use trait language in coaching your student writers.

Simply put, the traits are qualities or characteristics that define good writing. Following are definitions you can share with parents, if you wish:

The 6 Traits in a Nutshell

Trait 1

Ideas

Ideas are the heart of the message: the writer's main point or storyline, together with all the details that help make it clear and vivid for the reader.

Trait 2

Organization

Organization is the overall design or structure of the writing, including the lead (or beginning), the flow of ideas, the transitions connecting those ideas, and the conclusion (ending).

Trait 3

Voice

Voice is the writer's unique way of expressing ideas—the general sound and tone of the piece, the writer's presence in the text, the link between writer and reader, the verbal fingerprints of the writer on the page.

Trait 4

Word Choice

Word choice includes all the individual words, phrases, and expressions a writer uses to convey ideas and feelings.

Trait 5

Sentence Fluency

Sentence fluency is the flow and rhythm of the language, all the variations in sentence length and structure, and the degree to which text can be read easily and with expression.

Trait 6

Conventions

Conventions involve anything a copy editor would consider in making text easier to process, including (but not limited to) spelling, punctuation, grammar and usage, capitalization, paragraphing, spacing, and layout.

How are the lessons organized?

General Overview

In this collection, you will find **30 lessons** in all, **15 revision** lessons and **15 editing** lessons. They are alternated so that students practice revision, then editing, then revision again, and so on. Revision lessons are based on the five traits of *ideas, organization, voice, word choice*, and *sentence fluency*. Editing lessons are based on the trait of *conventions*.

Each **revision lesson** is designed to be completed within roughly **50 minutes**. Each **editing lesson** is designed to be completed within about **30–35 minutes**.

Revision lessons emphasize:

- Understanding of a foundational revision strategy
- Connection to literature
- A chance to see the strategy modeled (by the teacher)
- Collaboration between students
- Discussion, brainstorming, and sharing of ideas

Editing lessons emphasize:

- Direct instruction on one editorial concern
- Repeated practice on that editorial problem
- An opportunity to apply editorial skills

For writers who need extra time or practice . . .

All lessons in this set are designed for use with sixth grade writers and revisers. If you find a lesson is difficult for some students, you can adjust the amount of revising they do (e.g., making *a few small revisions* rather than dealing with the whole text). You can also break a revision lesson into two or three parts. Also remind students to read everything aloud as they go, and encourage students to work with partners *throughout the lesson.*

Connection to personal writing . . .

In all cases, the intent is that students move from the lesson to working on their own writing, applying the same revision or editing skills.

Specific Lesson Format and Timelines

For Revision Lessons

Preparing for a Revision Lesson To prepare, *read through the entire lesson.* Make any copies or overhead transparencies you need. Note that the format is the same for each lesson in the set. Once you are familiar with this format, the lesson flow is very easy, but of course, you should personalize each lesson *in any way you wish.*

Introducing a Revision Lesson Each revision lesson begins with (1) a short introduction describing the focus of the lesson and offering a relevant warm-up; and (2) a brief sample from literature or professional writing to help you illustrate an important writing feature: e.g., *revising by showing.*

Texts for individual lessons are short
The text for each revision lesson is deliberately kept short in order to make the lesson manageable for you. It is *not* intended to be fully representative of longer reports or essays your students may be writing. Unless otherwise directed, you should think of each sample as an *excerpt* from a potentially longer piece.

Teaching a Revision Lesson (with timelines) Revision lessons are designed to take about **50 minutes** (times will vary, depending on how much revising students do). Once you finish the Lesson Introduction, you have three options:

1. Do the lesson **all at once**
2. Divide the lesson into **two parts**
3. Divide the lesson into **three parts**

Regardless of which option you choose, the general flow goes like this:

Part 1

- Share Samples A and B.
- Discuss strengths and problems, and ask students what they might do to revise the *weaker* sample (**6–8 minutes**).
- *Optional:* Share and discuss our *suggested revision of the weaker sample* (**3 minutes**).

If you wish to divide the lesson into <u>3 parts</u>, pause here.

Part 2

- Share Sample C (*Whole Class Revision*).
- Read Sample C aloud as students follow along OR ask a student to read it aloud (**1 minute**).
- Invite students to work with a partner in identifying problems with Sample C, and to make notes they can use to coach you as you model revision of this sample (**6 minutes**).
- Invite students (as a class) to coach you as you model revision of Sample C (**6–8 minutes**). Read your revision aloud to close this portion of the lesson.
- *Optional:* Compare your whole class revision of Sample C with the suggested revision (**3 minutes**).

> If you wish to divide the lesson into 2 parts, pause here.
>
> If you are dividing the lesson into 3 parts, pause here for the second time.

Part 3

- Share Sample D (*Revising with Partners*).
- Ask students to revise Sample D independently, following the same strategies they used as a group for Sample C. Then, ask them to check with partners to compare strategies and results (**10–12 minutes**).
- Ask two or three pairs of students to share their revisions. The goal is to *hear some variations*, despite use of parallel strategies (**3–4 minutes**).
- *Optional:* Compare your revisions to our suggested revision of Sample D (**3 minutes**).

> ### How much revision should students do?
> The suggested revisions for *all* problematic pieces are provided to facilitate discussion and to give you models that show *possibilities*. Your revisions do not EVER need to match ours, and do not need to be as expansive as ours. Some students will revise *extensively*; beginners may do much less.

For Editing Lessons

Each **editing lesson** contains these basic components:

- Introduction and explanation of the focus skill for that lesson
- Illustrations you can share with students

- Instructions to guide you step by step through the lesson
- A sample for editing practice
- Edited copy that you can use as a model (for comparison) once students have finished their own editing

Teaching an editing lesson (with timelines) Allow about **30–35 minutes** for each editing lesson. Following is a brief estimate of how long each component is likely to take:

- Introduce the focus for the lesson (**3–4 minutes**).
- Share illustrations (**5–6 minutes**).
- Share the Editing Practice sample with students.
- Ask students to edit individually (**10–12 minutes**).
- Invite students to compare their editing with that of a partner (**3 minutes**).
- Invite students (as a class) to coach you as you model editing of the text (**5–6 minutes**). Read your edited copy aloud (**2 minutes**).
- Check your editing against the copy provided (**3 minutes**).

An editing checklist . . .
is provided with Lesson 30. You should feel free to share this checklist at any time during your use of these lessons. Simply realize that it may be challenging for students to apply the checklist until certain elements have been taught.

What if our changes do not agree with the suggested text?

In most cases, your editing should agree *very* closely with the copy provided. Admittedly, however, even widely used handbooks do not all agree on such issues as use of apostrophes in plurals. My suggestion is to choose one handbook that will be *your* final authority, and in the case of any disagreement, consult that handbook. In most cases, issues within editing lessons are noncontroversial, and disagreement should be minimal. (The resource text for this set of lessons is *The Chicago Manual of Style*, 14th edition. 1993. Chicago: University of Chicago Press. Also highly recommended: *Write Source New Generation for Grade 6*. 2006. Published by Great Source Education Group.)

With revision lessons, of course, there are no "correct" answers. What matters is that you and your students identify problems in the text and revise them in a way that makes the draft clear and readable. The suggested revisions are provided *to guide you*, to make you aware of possibilities, and also to make you more comfortable discussing samples or modeling revision. They are not meant to restrict what you can or should do as writers and revisers.

Do these lessons fit well into writing workshop?

Absolutely! Usually, writing workshop offers a combination of direct instruction, coaching, writing and revising, and sharing. These lessons provide excellent opportunities for direct instruction and coaching, while allowing students the support of working in pairs or teams, as well as connecting reading and writing. Because they are designed to help students become independent editors and revisers, with a strong grasp of writers' vocabulary, these lessons fit very well into any writing workshop that encourages students to take charge of their own writing process. They are *not* meant to take the place of students' independent writing. Rather, they serve as a stepping stone into that writing—giving students just the strategies they need to make both drafting and revising stronger.

What can I do to make these lessons more effective?

Many things. Here are 15 suggestions—

1. **Read *Creating Writers Through 6-Trait Assessment and Revision*,** Fifth Edition (2009. Boston: Pearson Education), for grades 3 through college, and keep a copy handy to refer to as you use these lessons.

2. **Make sure students have access to handbooks** (e.g., *Write Source New Generation,* published by Great Source Education), dictionaries, and thesauruses. Provide space on which to post a traits checklist or other lists and charts used throughout the lessons (You will need to make your own enlarged copies).

3. At any time you feel it is appropriate during your presentation of these revision lessons, **provide students with copies of the Student 6-Point Writing Guide**. Also provide copies of the **Student Checklist** (both at the end of the Introduction). Students can use the **Writing Guide** and/or **Checklist** as a guide in assessing any writing (including their own) *prior to revision*. These materials are *not essential for completing the lessons* in the set, but they give additional reinforcement in defining what it means to write well, and also provide a strong link to the *Creating Writers* text.

4. **Do not assess *everything*** students create. It will be overwhelming for both them and you. Also, do not evaluate the work they do in conjunction with these lessons except in the sense that they *complete* all revision and editing activities. Think of the lessons as rehearsal for their own personal writing.

5. **Allow extended writing time.** Encourage students to keep folders of their own writing, and to occasionally choose a draft of their own work to revise, applying strategies learned from this lesson set. Recognize that both writing and revising are reflective activities that require time, some of which should be provided in class, where student writers have access to resources and to coaching from peers and from you.

6. **When students have written a draft, let them "abandon" it mentally for a time** by putting it into the writing folder, and doing nothing more with it for three or more days. During this time, present one or more revision/editing lessons. When students return to their drafts, they will see their writing with fresh eyes, and will have in their minds specific skills to apply as they revise. The difference will impress you—and encourage them.

7. **Remind students to double space their own rough drafts,** and to leave large side margins, providing room for revision and editorial notes. Even if they work on computers, encourage them to format drafts in this way. That way, they can make notes on printed copy to guide the revision they later do electronically.

8. **Keep revision small and focused.** Changing one sentence or inserting one or two details is a good beginning for some students. Encourage experimentation. Do not expect students to do as much revision as you will see in our examples. Those are provided for discussion purposes to help you and your students see various possibilities. There is *no expectation* that any one student will make *every possible revision.*

9. **Adapt lessons for challenged writers.** Because the lessons focus on one aspect of revision, they are already fairly manageable in scope. But you can make them simpler still by (1) asking students who are having difficulty to make only *one* small change, rather than focusing on a full paragraph or page; (2) ensuring that any student who is struggling has a partner with whom to work, even during those times when other students may be working independently; (3) encouraging struggling students to talk through their ideas for revision before putting anything on paper; and (4) using the recommended literature to provide models (sentences, words, phrases, images, details) that students can refer to or even copy verbatim.

10. **Challenge those writers who are ready.** Every lesson concludes with a section called "Next Steps," which includes suggestions for "writers who need a challenge."

11. **Seat students in a way that makes working in pairs (or larger teams) easy and comfortable**.

12. **Write with your students,** modeling the kinds of things you would like them to do, such as double spacing copy, changing an ending, starting sentences differently, or inserting a word or phrase you like better than your original.

13. **Share additional examples from good literature** with your students. One brief example is provided in each lesson, but if you can provide more examples from that and other recommended texts, you make the use of literary mentors even more powerful.

14. **Make yourself as comfortable as possible with the modeling process.** You will have a suggested revision to review in advance, and you can use that suggestion to guide students' responses. However, your final draft need not look like ours. Feel free to be inventive, and to encourage creativity in your students. What matters is for them to see the revision unfold.

15. **Help students understand that the kind of revision they do within these lessons is *a beginning*.** The author of a published book might revise a manuscript fifteen times—or more. The purpose of these lessons is not to create publishable drafts. The purpose is to practice *revision and editing strategies*. On their own, your students will *eventually* go much further than the lessons suggest, and will combine many strategies in revising a given document.

Have fun watching your students' revision and editing skills grow!

Checklists
Creating Revisers and Editors, Grade 6

Note to the Teacher

Following is a series of checklists intended for use with this set of lessons. Use the checklists one at a time, as you are teaching the lessons for a particular trait—or pass them all out at once. It's your choice. Here are a few things to keep in mind . . .

Encourage honesty! Good writers make *numerous changes* to their text. So in filling out a checklist, the object is not to show how *perfect* your writing is, but to be such a good reader (of your own work) that you know how to tackle revision. Remind students that most early drafts—even those written by professionals—would *not* meet all the criteria listed here. A good checklist is a guide to revision, a series of reminders.

Keep revision manageable. Once students have more than one checklist going, it is a good idea to think about how many things the writer wants to take on at once. Addressing one or two writer's problems thoroughly can improve a draft measurably. This is sufficient for struggling writers. Students who are ready for a challenge may wish to try doing more than one revision of a given draft.

A Writing Guide is different from a checklist. A writing guide includes *numbers*, and shows a writer where his or her writing falls along a continuum of performance from beginning levels up to strong and proficient. A *6-Trait Writing Guide* is provided with these lessons. It corresponds to the guide found in *Creating Writers,* Fifth Edition. Students can use it (1) to score the writing of anonymous writers (such as those whose work appears in these lessons), or (2) to score their own writing *in preparation for revision—not* for grading purposes.

Remember that the purpose of these lessons is to create *revisers*, not *critics*. The discussion that comes out of assessing a piece of work and talking about it with others is extremely helpful in giving writers the insight they need to do their work better. But a checklist will often serve that purpose well without the need for a score.

Organization

— A strong lead invites you in

— A strong ending wraps things up

— Every detail seems to fall in the right place

— My organization guides readers like a good road map

— It's not *too* predictable—it includes some surprises

— I show how ideas connect

— The pacing is just right—not too fast or too slow

© Vicki Spandel, 2009. Excerpt from *Creating Writers Through 6-Trait Writing Assessment and Instruction*, Fifth Edition. Pearson Education, Inc. All rights reserved.

Ideas

— Everything is clear—it makes sense

— Examples expand my main idea

— I know this topic well—and it shows

— I include helpful, memorable, intriguing details

— It's more than just a list of facts

— My writing answers reader's questions

— I include what matters—NOT filler!

— My writing makes readers think

© Vicki Spandel, 2009. Excerpt from *Creating Writers Through 6-Trait Writing Assessment and Instruction*, Fifth Edition. Pearson Education, Inc. All rights reserved.

Word Choice

___ Every word and expression is "just right" for the moment

___ The writing is original and creative—I say things *my own way*

___ Words are used accurately

___ New or technical words are defined

___ The writing makes vivid pictures, movies in the reader's mind

___ Lively verbs put things into motion

___ Adjectives and adverbs aren't *overused*

___ Every word counts—I didn't use 20 words when 10 would do

© Vicki Spandel, 2009. Excerpt from *Creating Writers Through 6-Trait Writing Assessment and Instruction*, Fifth Edition. Pearson Education, Inc. All rights reserved.

Voice

___ It's individual—my fingerprints are on *every page*

___ The writing is expressive—you can tell I like this topic

___ The tone and language create the right mood

___ My knowledge of the topic gives the writing conviction

___ This piece speaks to readers

___ You'll enjoy reading it aloud

___ This is the right voice for the genre and purpose

© Vicki Spandel, 2009. Excerpt from *Creating Writers Through 6-Trait Writing Assessment and Instruction*, Fifth Edition. Pearson Education, Inc. All rights reserved.

Please note . . .

No checklist is included for Conventions because it appears in conjunction with the editing lessons.

Personal Revision Guide

Sentence Fluency

—— This writing is easy and fun to read aloud—*with expression*

—— Some sentences are long, some short

—— Sentences begin in different ways

—— Many sentence beginnings link ideas with transitions like . . . *After a while, Nevertheless, Moreover, For example, On the other hand, The next day . . .*

—— I used fragments or repetition only for *emphasis*

—— Dialogue (if used) sounds authentic and natural

© Vicki Spandel, 2009. Excerpt from *Creating Writers Through 6-Trait Writing Assessment and Instruction,* Fifth Edition. Pearson Education, Inc. All rights reserved.

Student Writing Guide, Grade 6

Ideas

6
- My writing is clear and focused—it will hold your attention.
- I know this topic inside and out.
- I help readers learn—and make them think, imagine, envision.
- Out of many possibilities, I chose the *most intriguing* details.

5
- My writing is clear and focused.
- I know a lot about this topic.
- I share information that matters—to me and to my readers.
- I include many helpful details and examples.

4
- My paper is clear and focused most of the time.
- I know this topic well enough to write about it.
- My paper has some new information.
- I came up with a few details and examples.

3
- I ran out of things to say. Not every part is clear, either.
- I wish I knew more about this topic!
- It was hard to come up with new information.
- I scrambled for details. I think I repeated some things.

2
- I have a topic—*sort of*—but I'm not sure what to say about it.
- I did not know enough to write about this topic.
- I made my best guesses—or just repeated things.
- I listed some ideas—but I didn't have any good details or examples.

1
- I don't have a real topic. I'm not sure what to say.
- Without a topic, how could I have information?
- I just wrote whatever came into my head.
- I wrote what I could. It isn't really *about anything* in particular.

Organization

6
- My organization guides you right through the piece.
- My lead will hook you. My conclusion will leave you thinking.
- I link ideas in ways you might not think of on your own.
- The overall design gives a real sense of purpose to my writing.

5
- The organization helps you focus on what's most important.
- I have a strong lead and a conclusion that wraps things up.
- My transitions connect ideas clearly—you don't have to make your own connections.
- The organization makes everything easy to follow.

4
- The organization supports the ideas.
- I have a lead and conclusion. They seem OK.
- My transitions link ideas pretty clearly.
- You can follow it—but sometimes you know what's coming next.

3
- If you pay attention, you can follow my story or discussion.
- My lead and/or conclusion need some work.
- You'll need to make some connections as you read this. Or else, use the old formulas: *point one, point two, etc.*
- It's either hard to follow—or else REALLY predictable!

2
- I feel like reorganizing *everything*—beginning to end!
- My lead and conclusion are the same ones you've heard before.
- I wasn't sure how to connect these ideas. I need to think about it.
- This is very hard to follow even if you pay attention.

1
- This seems totally random—there's no pattern or design here.
- It just starts and stops. There's no lead or conclusion.
- These ideas don't really go together. They're just first thoughts.
- No one can follow this. I can't follow it myself.

Copyright ©2009. Pearson Education, Inc. *Creating Revisers and Editors.* Vicki Spandel. All rights reserved. May be used only in a classroom context. All other uses prohibited.

Student Writing Guide, Grade 6

Voice

6
- ☐ This is ME—as individual as my fingerprints.
- ☐ Trust me—you *will* want to share this aloud.
- ☐ I use voice to make the message resonate in your head.
- ☐ Hear the passion? I want you to love this topic as much as I do.

5
- ☐ It's original and distinctive. It will definitely stand out from the crowd.
- ☐ I think you will want to read this aloud.
- ☐ The voice fits my topic. I reach out to the audience.
- ☐ The paper is lively and expressive. I liked this topic.

4
- ☐ My writing strikes a spark or two. You *might* recognize me.
- ☐ You might share a line or two aloud.
- ☐ Though my voice fades at times, you can tell I'm thinking of the reader.
- ☐ This paper is sincere. This was an OK topic for me.

3
- ☐ My voice comes and goes. I'm not sure you could tell it's me.
- ☐ There could be a share-aloud moment in there somewhere.
- ☐ I wasn't *always* thinking of the reader. I just wrote.
- ☐ My voice is quiet in this paper. I couldn't really get into this topic.

2
- ☐ This isn't really me. It's more of an "anybody" voice.
- ☐ There could be a hint of voice in one or two moments.
- ☐ My voice is faint—just a whisper, really.
- ☐ I sound bored—or like an encyclopedia. This was NOT my topic.

1
- ☐ I'm not at home in this paper. I can't hear myself at all.
- ☐ This is definitely not a piece to share aloud.
- ☐ My voice is just—well, *missing* . . . Not even a whisper . . .
- ☐ I couldn't get excited about the topic. You won't either.

Word Choice

6
- ☐ I tried for original, creative ways to use words.
- ☐ You might read this more than once—you'll remember a phrase or two.
- ☐ Every word is important. I wouldn't cut anything.
- ☐ I used strong verbs—and precise nouns and adjectives.
- ☐ My words make vivid, memorable pictures in your mind.

5
- ☐ I wrote to make meaning clear—not to impress you.
- ☐ Once you start reading, you'll want to keep reading.
- ☐ I kept it concise.
- ☐ I used strong verbs. I didn't overdo the adjectives.
- ☐ My words help you picture things clearly.

4
- ☐ My writing is clear. I used words correctly.
- ☐ You'll notice some strong words or phrases.
- ☐ I could cut a little.
- ☐ There are some strong verbs—also vague words (*nice, fun, great*).
- ☐ My writing gives you the general picture.

3
- ☐ I used the first words that came to me—but you'll get the idea.
- ☐ Here and there is a word or phrase I like.
- ☐ It's a little cluttery. I should shorten it.
- ☐ I need more strong verbs. Many words are vague or general.
- ☐ You'll need to use your imagination—or fill in some blanks.

2
- ☐ Watch out for tired words, vague words, or thesaurus overload!
- ☐ You'll have to look hard to find strong moments.
- ☐ It's very sketchy—or else it's so overdone the message is lost.
- ☐ Strong verbs rode into the sunset. I might have too many adjectives.
- ☐ You'll have to work hard just to get the main idea.

1
- ☐ I wrote to fill space. I don't think any message comes through.
- ☐ It was a struggle to get *anything* on paper.
- ☐ I need more words, stronger words, *different* words—help!!

Copyright ©2009. Pearson Education, Inc. *Creating Revisers and Editors.* Vicki Spandel. All rights reserved. May be used only in a classroom context. All other uses prohibited.

Student Writing Guide, Grade 6

Sentence Fluency

6
- This is easy to read with expression and voice.
- It flows like a good song lyric or movie script.
- You won't believe the variety in my sentences.
- If I used fragments, they add punch. My dialogue is like listening in on a good conversation.

5
- You can read this with expression.
- It has a good rhythm and flow. I like the sound of it.
- My sentences begin in different ways. Some are long, some short.
- Fragments or repetition add emphasis. Dialogue sounds real.

4
- My writing sounds natural. It's easy to read aloud.
- It flows for the most part. I might smooth out a wrinkle or two.
- I have some sentence variety. I could use more.
- Fragments or repetition sound OK. My dialogue could use some work—it's pretty natural, though.

3
- If you read this aloud, it's a bumpy ride. You can do it, though.
- I need to read this aloud myself and rewrite some sentences.
- I need MUCH more sentence variety.
- My fragments (if I used them) don't work. The dialogue doesn't quite sound like real people speaking.

2
- You can read this if you're patient—and you rehearse!
- I have run-ons, choppy sentences, or other sentence problems.
- My sentences are all alike—or it's hard to tell where they start.
- If I used fragments or repetition, it was by accident.

1
- This is very *hard* to read aloud, even for me.
- You need to re-read a lot—or fill in missing words as you go.
- It's hard to tell where sentences start or stop.
- I need to read this aloud, slowly. I need to rewrite sentences, finish sentences, and combine some sentences.

Conventions

6
- I edited this thoroughly. Only the pickiest editors will spot errors.
- My conventions are creative. They bring out meaning and voice.
- This paper shows off my control over many conventions.
- *If layout was important*, I made it appealing and eye-catching. This is **ready to publish.**

5
- I edited this. Errors are minor and easy to overlook.
- My conventions support the meaning and voice.
- The paper shows I know many different conventions.
- *If layout was important*, I made sure the piece had a pleasing look. This is ready to publish with **light touchups.**

4
- I went through it quickly. There are a few noticeable errors.
- It's very readable. The errors do not get in the way of the message.
- I have good control over basics—*end punctuation, capitals,* etc.
- *If layout was important*, I made sure it was acceptable. This piece needs **a good once-over** before it's published.

3
- I edited too quickly. This has noticeable, distracting errors.
- The errors could slow a reader down—or get in the way of meaning.
- Even with basics (like *easy spelling*) I had some problems.
- This needs more attention to layout (*optional*). This piece needs **careful, thorough editing** before it's published.

2
- Frequent, distracting errors show it's not really edited yet.
- The errors will slow a reader down—or distort the meaning.
- I made many errors, even on basics.
- I did not think too much about layout (*optional*). This needs **line-by-line editing** before it's published.

1
- This is not edited. There are serious, frequent errors.
- Readers will need to de-code or reread to get the meaning.
- I made many errors, even on basics like *periods and capitals.*
- I need to re-work the layout (*optional*). This needs **word-by-word editing** before it's published.

Copyright ©2009. Pearson Education, Inc. *Creating Revisers and Editors.* Vicki Spandel. All rights reserved. May be used only in a classroom context. All other uses prohibited.

Bibliography

List of Books Referenced for Grade 6 Lesson Set

Barry, Dave and Ridley Pearson. *Peter and the Secret of Rundoon.* 2007. New York: Hyperion (Disney Editions).

Barry, Dave and Ridley Pearson. 2004. *Peter and the Starcatchers.* New York: Hyperion.

Beard, Daniel Carter. *American Boy's Handy Book: What to Do and How to Do It, Centennial Edition.* 1998. New York: David R. Godine.

Beard, Lina. *American Girls Handy Book: How to Amuse Yourself and Others.* 1994. New York: David R. Godine.

Brooks, Bruce. *Nature by Design.* 1991. New York: Farrar, Straus, and Giroux.

Brooks, Bruce. *Predator!* 1991. New York: Farrar, Straus, and Giroux.

Buchanan, Andrea J. and Mirian Peskowitz.*The Daring Book for Girls.* 2007. New York: HarperCollins.

Burns, Loree Griffin.*Tracking Trash: Flotsam, Jetsam, and the Science of Ocean Motion.* 2007. Boston: Houghton Mifflin.

Cisneros, Sandra. *The House on Mango Street.* 1991. New York: Vintage.

Codell, Esmé Raji. *Sahara Special.* 2004. New York: Hyperion.

Codell, Esmé Raji. *Sing a Song of Tuna Fish.* 2004. New York: Hyperion Paperbacks for Children.

Collard, Sneed B. III. *Pocket Babies and Other Amazing Marsupials.* 2007. Plain City, OH: Darby Creek Publishing.

Collard, Sneed B. *The Prairie Builders.* 2005. Boston: Houghton Mifflin.

Dahl, Roald. *The BFG.* 2007. New York: Puffin.

Dahl, Roald. *Boy.* 1999. New York: Puffin.

DiCamillo, Kate. *The Miraculous Journey of Edward Toulane.* 2006. Cambridge, MA: Candlewick Press.

Dowell, Frances O'Roark. *Dovey Coe.* 2001. New York: Aladdin.

Enright, Dominique and Guy Macdonald. *How to Be the Best at Everything (The Boys' Book).* 2007. New York: Scholastic.

Foster, Juliana. *How to Be the Best at Everything (The Girls' Book).* 2007. New York: Scholastic.

Gantos, Jack. *Jack's Black Book.* 1999. New York: Farrar, Straus, and Giroux.

Glausiusz, Josie. *Buzz: The Intimate Bond Between Humans and Insects.* 2004. San Francisco: Chronicle Books.

Gordon, David George. *The Compleat Cockroach*. 1996. Berkeley, CA: Ten Speed Press.

Iggulden, Conn and Hal Iggulden. *The Dangerous Book for Boys*. 2007. New York: HarperCollins.

Karg, Barb and Rick Sutherland, eds. *Letters to My Teacher: Tributes to the People Who Have Made a Difference*. 2006. Avon, MA: Adams Media.

Karr, Kathleen. *Exiled: Memoirs of a Camel*. 2006. Tarrytown, NY: Marshall Cavendish.

Korman, Gordon. *No More Dead Dogs*. 2000. New York: Hyperion Books.

Kramer, Stephen. *Hidden Worlds: Looking Through a Scientist's Microscope*. 2001. Boston: Houghton Mifflin.

Kurlansky, Mark. *The Story of Salt*. 2006. New York: G. P. Putnam's Sons.

Lord, Cynthia. *Rules*. 2006. New York: Scholastic.

Martin, Ann M. *A Dog's Life*. 2005. New York: Scholastic.

Miller, Sarah. *Miss Spitfire*. 2007. New York: Atheneum.

Murphy, Jim. *Blizzard*. 2000. New York: Scholastic.

Paulsen, Gary. *Dogteam*. 1995. New York: Dragonfly Books.

Paulsen, Gary. *Hatchet: 20th Anniversary Edition*. 2007. New York: Simon and Schuster.

Sachar, Louis. *Holes*. 1998. New York: Random House.

Schmidt, Gary D. *Lizzie Bright and the Buckminster Boy*. 2006. New York: Yearling.

Schmidt, Gary D. *The Wednesday Wars*. 2007. New York: Clarion Books.

Schusterman, Neal. *The Schwa Was Here*. 2004. New York: Penguin Books.

Selznick, Brian. *The Invention of Hugo Cabret*. 2007. New York: Scholastic.

Spinelli, Jerry. *Maniac Magee*. 2002. New York: Scholastic.

Woodford, Chris and Luke Collins, Clint Witchalls, Ben Morgan, and James Flint. *Cool Stuff and How It Works*. 2005. New York: DK Publishing.

Lessons for Grade 6

*Indicates editing lesson.

Revising a Character Sketch

Trait Connection: **Ideas**

Introduction

Suppose someone was asked to describe you, and that description had to be so accurate, so spot on, that no one could get you mixed up with anyone else in the world. What would be the top three things that person would mention? If you can come up with three (or more), you know the secret to a good character sketch: it's capturing the details that distinguish an individual. Sometimes those details are physical characteristics—bushy eyebrows or a mole on the chin. Sometimes they are ways of moving or speaking. And sometimes, they're about personality—the things that make a person laugh or cry, or the way he or she sees the world. If you tend to notice the little things that make an individual unique, you've got what it takes to write good character sketches.

Teacher's Sidebar . . .
Skillful character sketches nearly always include a *little* physical detail, but it's often a detail connected to personality—hair that hides a face, for example. In the best sketches, the character speaks or does something that reveals who he or she is *inside*. We know a sketch has been successful when, as readers, we can say, "I feel as if I *know* her (or him)."

Focus and Intent

This lesson is intended to help students:

- Identify the kinds of descriptive clues that make for a good character sketch.
- Distinguish between strong—and not so strong—character sketches.
- Revise a general character sketch to make the person seem real.

Teaching the Lesson

Step 1: Design a Character

Put students into teams of two, and ask them to design a character by brainstorming answers to each of the following questions and recording their answers on a half sheet of paper. Allow *no more than 7 minutes* (one minute per question). Students need to think and write quickly!

1. *What is the character's name?* _____

   Does he/she like this name? _____

2. *How old is this person?* _____

3. *What are the person's hobbies or interests?* _____

4. *Who or what does the person love most?* _____

5. *What is one thing this person fears?*

   _____

6. *If you met this person for the first time, what would you notice first?*

   _____

7. *Deep inside his/her heart, what is this person wishing or hoping for?*

   _____

When students have finished, ask them to exchange answer sheets with another team—and to create a five-sentence sketch of the character, based on the information they're given on the sheet. It is *not* necessary to include *every detail* from the original design in these sketches. And, it is fine to invent new information. When you finish, read and discuss some sketches. What information did writers find most helpful? What new information did they need to think up on their own?

Step 2: Making the Reading-Writing Connection

When author Roald Dahl was seven, he and his friends routinely visited a candy shop (called a sweet shop) in Llandaff, the town where he lived outside of London. Following is Dahl's description of the woman who ran that sweet shop. Do you like her? On a scale of 1 to 10, how likely would *you* be to visit her store?

Sample

Her name was Mrs Pratchett. She was a small skinny old hag with a moustache on her upper lip and a mouth as sour as a green gooseberry. She never smiled. She never welcomed us when we went in, and the only times she spoke were when she said things like, "I'm watchin' you so keep yer thievin' fingers off them chocolates!" Or "I don't want you in 'ere just to look around! Either you forks out or you gets out!"

(From Dahl, Roald. *Boy*. 1999. New York: Puffin.)

Close your eyes and picture Mrs Pratchett. What do you see? What specific details give us clues about Mrs Pratchett's personality? What do we learn about her from the way she speaks? Though Roald Dahl doesn't tell us, how tall do you suppose Mrs Pratchett is? How old is she? What sort of shoes does she wear? Do you think she wears jewelry or makeup? Notice that writers always leave some details to our imagination. Do they do this on purpose? Suppose Roald Dahl had written, "Mrs Pratchett was a really mean old lady." Would this have the same effect? Why?

Step 3: Involving Students as Evaluators

Ask students to review Samples A and B, each of which offers a character sketch based on the same person. *Which sketch best reveals what Uncle Ollie is really like?* Have students work with a partner, highlighting clues from each sketch that reveal character, and then identifying the stronger one.

Discussing Results

Most students should find Sample B stronger. Discuss differences between the two sketches, asking students to identify specific details that make Sketch B more vivid—and make Uncle Ollie seem like a real person. What is Uncle Ollie like? What words describe him?

Step 4: Modeling Revision

- Share Sample C (*Whole Class Revision*) with students. Read the original aloud—perhaps more than once.

- Talk about Mrs. Cutter. Are the clues to her personality vivid—or too general? What is Mrs. Cutter really like?

- Brainstorm which character traits to focus on—and how to bring them to life. Don't forget the importance of having a character speak.

- Revise the sketch by making Mrs. Cutter seem real—give her personality. Let her breathe. Let the reader in on how she feels. *Note:* Feel free to invent any details you wish.

Step 5: Revising with Partners

Pass out copies of Sample D (*Revising with Partners*). Ask students to follow the basic steps you modeled with Sample C. *Working with partners,* they should:

- Read the passage aloud—more than once if that is helpful.

- Discuss Isaiah's main traits—What makes him tick?

- Revise by first talking through the little clues that would reveal Isaiah's character—and then writing them out in their own words.

- Read the result aloud to see if they have brought the character to life.

Step 6: Sharing and Discussing Results

When students have finished, ask several pairs of students to share their revisions aloud. Did teams choose a range of ways to reveal character? Did all revisions reflect the same basic character traits, or is Isaiah a different person in each sketch? Did any teams choose to have Isaiah speak?

Next Steps

■ The introduction to this lesson asks students to answer a series of seven questions—but there are many more questions that could be important in revealing character. Invite students to work with you in creating a "character inventory"—a list of questions they feel are key in showing who someone really is. Post it—and add to it now and then.

■ Try applying your character inventory to an actual character from literature. Then consider how the writer makes these various traits clear.

■ Collect postcards of striking but unrecognizable faces (no one from current pop culture or well-known history). Ask students to draw a card at random and to keep the card with them for two or three days, studying the face and imagining who the person behind that face really is. Ask them to create a short character sketch or first-person journal entry revealing who is in the picture. Make a book of the class results.

■ Most characters are revealed over time, through a whole story or book. Yet, that first impression is important. Watch and listen for first introductions in the literature you share. Recommended:

● *Boy* by Roald Dahl. 1999. New York: Puffin. (In addition to Mrs Pratchett, check out "The Matron" in the chapter of that title.)

● *Peter and the Starcatchers* by Dave Barry and Ridley Pearson. 2004. New York: Hyperion. (Meet the infamous Black Stache in Chapter 4.)

● *Sahara Special* by Esmé Raji Codell. 2004. New York: Hyperion. (Say hello to the new teacher in Chapter 5.)

■ *For an additional challenge:* Ask students to create a character sketch based on someone from their own family—but to add details they had not thought of before. They might collect those details from a photo album, observations, conversations—or even an interview. If the person is deceased, another relative or friend may be able to fill in some blanks. Invite students to present their character sketches (with photos, if possible) to the class.

Sample A: Uncle Ollie

Vivid clues?
or
Generalities?

Uncle Ollie was an older man. He walked with a bit of a limp. He had gray hair. He liked to eat. He also liked to drive. He drove an old Chevrolet. Ollie drove himself to the Post Office each day, even in bad weather. Once he drove Aunt Edna to the Post Office on icy roads. They had to clear snow off the windshield first. Edna was a little nervous, but Ollie just told her not to worry, and off they went.

©2009. Allyn & Bacon, a division of Pearson Education. Developed by Vicki Spandel. All rights reserved.

Sample B: Uncle Ollie

Vivid clues?
or
Generalities?

Uncle Ollie was a gray-haired, red-faced stamp collector, who walked with a bit of a limp—which he kept hidden under a long, woolly coat. He loved jelly doughnuts, or nearly anything else edible, and nibbled constantly, like a grazing animal. Ollie drove an old Chevrolet that had never been serviced or washed. He had no license and probably could not have passed the test. He didn't fret over it. Tests seemed optional.

One winter, when Aunt Edna was desperate to go to the Post Office, she hesitated to ask Ollie, unsure if retrieving mail was worth her life. He slapped on his hat and coat before she could think up a proper excuse. The roads were so icy they nearly fell twice just walking from the front door to the old Chevy—which was caked with snow, bumper to bumper. Ollie used the end of a rolled newspaper to clear a peek-a-boo opening on the glass, just over the steering wheel. "Aren't you going to clear the *whole* windshield?" Edna asked hopefully.

Ollie laughed and slapped the knee of his good leg. "Heavens, no! What for? Get in, Edna!" he shouted, hurling himself into the driver's seat. Off they went, Edna clinging to the dash board, her hat askew.

©2009. Allyn & Bacon, a division of Pearson Education. Developed by Vicki Spandel. All rights reserved.

Sample C: Whole Class Revision

Vivid clues?
or
Generalities?

Mrs. Cutter

Mrs. Cutter was a neat, careful person. She had worked in the library for a long, long time. She liked her job. She took good care of the library. She kept it tidy. It wasn't always easy. People were always taking books off the shelves and putting them somewhere. It bothered Mrs. Cutter a lot. Sometimes, she just had to speak up!

©2009. Allyn & Bacon, a division of Pearson Education. Developed by Vicki Spandel. All rights reserved.

Sample D: Revising with Partners

Vivid clues?
or
Generalities?

Isaiah

Isaiah had dark hair and dark eyes. He was the oldest of four children. Sometimes he liked that and sometimes not.

Isaiah liked to dress a little differently from other kids. He said it was good to be different.

Though he was not tall, Isaiah was strong. He was also a good runner. Isaiah liked to say he could win just about any race.

©2009. Allyn & Bacon, a division of Pearson Education. Developed by Vicki Spandel. All rights reserved.

Suggested Revisions of C and D

Sample C: Whole Class Revision

Mrs. Cutter

never had a strand of hair out of place or a button unbuttoned.
Mrs. Cutter ~~was a neat, careful person~~ She had worked in

longer than most people had been on planet Earth and loved
the library ~~for a long, long time. She liked~~ her job. She ~~took~~

cared for the library as if it were her own home, dusting and polishing
~~good care of the library. She kept it tidy~~ It wasn't always   every inch.

Pesky   yanking   her newly dusted
easy. People were always ~~taking~~ books off ~~the~~ shelves and

hiding   in some faraway corner.   gave   roaring headache!
~~putting~~ them ~~somewhere~~ It ~~bothered~~ Mrs. Cutter a ~~lot~~

found herself whispering, "Go make a mess in your own home!"
Sometimes, she ~~just had to speak up!~~ She felt like

shouting, but after all, it was the library. Usually, if

she stared at them long enough through her rimless

glasses, they slunk away.

©2009. Allyn & Bacon, a division of Pearson Education. Developed by Vicki Spandel. All rights reserved.

Sample D: Revising with Partners

Isaiah

Isaiah had ~~dark~~ hair and dark eyes. He was the oldest of *[the color of a raven's wing]* *[that peered right into your soul.]*

four children. Sometimes he liked ~~that~~ and sometimes ~~not~~ *[being the one in charge,]*

he wished he could escape to an empty rooftop or back lot.

Isaiah ~~liked to dress a little differently from other~~ *[always wore something orange—a hat, socks, or whatever.]*

~~kids. He said it was good to be different.~~ *[liked to say that being different was just another way]* *[of being yourself.]*

Though he was not tall, Isaiah was strong. *[enough to lift 100 pounds right over his head.]*

He was also a good runner. ~~Isaiah liked to say he could win~~ *["Race me if you dare," he'd say. "I can run the shoes right off your feet."]*

~~just about any race.~~

©2009. Allyn & Bacon, a division of Pearson Education. Developed by Vicki Spandel. All rights reserved.

Commas in a Series

Trait Connection: **Conventions**

Introduction (Share with students in your own words.)

Commas are used to separate items in a series—such as items you are packing in your suitcase or things Aunt Jane puts into her special soup:

I packed a <u>toothbrush</u>, <u>razor</u>, and <u>comb</u>.

Aunt Jane's soup recipe calls for <u>eels</u>, <u>snails</u>, and <u>eggplant</u>.

Elements in a series aren't always nouns (*things*), of course. Sometimes they're phrases, like these *prepositional phrases* that show *where* the bat flew:

The bat flew <u>over our heads</u>, <u>across the yard</u>, and <u>through the trees</u>.

Commas can also separate a series of events or actions:

Aunt Jane <u>dried her eyes</u>, <u>packed up her soup pot</u>, and <u>vowed never to cook</u> for us again.

And sometimes a series comes at the beginning of a sentence instead of at the end:

<u>Snow</u>, <u>wind</u>, and <u>hail</u> all hit on the same day.

Some people (we're not naming names) believe it's OK to omit the final comma in a series, provided the sentence is clear without it:

Please add spinach, bread and mayonnaise to the shopping list.
(Notice that there is no comma after bread.)

Other editors disagree, though, and prefer to leave that final comma in. We'll use that rule (final comma in place) for this editing practice so that there is no confusion. To insert a comma, just use an editor's caret, and tuck the comma right inside:

Della ate four doughnuts‸ two chicken legs‸ and a whole cake. That's a lot for a beagle.

Teaching the Lesson (General Guidelines for Teachers)

1. Share the preceding examples, or make up your own examples to practice using commas in a series.

2. Share the editing lesson on the following page. Students should read the passage aloud, looking and listening for needed commas and inserting them to separate all elements in each series.

3. Ask them to edit individually first, then check with a partner.

4. When everyone is done, ask them to coach you as you edit the same copy.

5. When you finish, read your edited copy aloud; then compare it with our suggested text on page 34.

6. If you wish, set up your own classroom rule about commas in a series, specifying whether you wish your student editors to follow the next-to-last element with a comma, or do not care about observing that rule.

Editing Goal: Fill in 11 missing commas.
Follow-Up: Check for correct use of commas in a series
when editing your own work.

Editing Practice

Insert missing commas.

Uncle Reuben's dark and dingy basement was plagued by rats mice and spiders. Poor Reuben had tried brooms flyswatters traps and even poison. *Nothing* worked! He felt fed up exhausted and dismayed by the whole thing. What should he do? Keep trying the same old remedies? Give up? Finally, he built a fire made himself some tea and sat down in his easy chair to think. "Got it!" he exclaimed a few minutes later. The next day, he brought home a cat who was remarkably crafty extremely ferocious and outrageously hungry.

©2009. Allyn & Bacon, a division of Pearson Education. Developed by Vicki Spandel. All rights reserved.

Edited Copy

11 missing commas inserted

Uncle Reuben's dark and dingy basement was plagued by rats, mice, and spiders. Poor Reuben had tried brooms, flyswatters, traps, and even poison. *Nothing* worked! He felt fed up, exhausted, and dismayed by the whole thing. What should he do? Keep trying the same old remedies? Give up? Finally, he built a fire, made himself some tea, and sat down in his easy chair to think. "Got it!" he exclaimed a few minutes later. The next day, he brought home a cat who was remarkably crafty, extremely ferocious, and outrageously hungry.

©2009. Allyn & Bacon, a division of Pearson Education. Developed by Vicki Spandel. All rights reserved.

Revising with the 5 W's

Trait Connection: **Ideas**

Introduction

The so-called 5 W's—*Who, What, Where, When,* and *Why*—are usually associated with journalism, or news writing. They're very useful, however, in checking the thoroughness of informational writing, too. *Who* refers to any person—or other being—central to the information at hand. *What* refers to the story (as in "What happened?") or to the topic—what the article is about, and the facts or details the writer uses to support and expand the main idea. *Where* can refer to a specific place, such as Venice, Italy, or to a much broader setting, like *anywhere* U.S.A., or even planet Earth itself. *When* might refer to a specific date, a time period, or the present. *Why* refers to the reason behind an event—why it's significant or why we find it interesting. Good informational writers address *most* of the 5 W's *most* of the time. However, they may take several paragraphs or even an entire book to do so. In this lesson, we'll condense things a bit so we can hit all five within a paragraph or two.

Teacher's Sidebar . . .

Journalistic writing emphasizes inclusion of the 5 W's within the first sentence or two of a news story. The purpose in this lesson is a little different: to use the 5 W's as a way of checking whether all important information has been included—or as a helpful way of planning an informational piece.

Focus and Intent

This lesson is intended to help students:

- Understand what the 5 W's are.
- Recognize the 5 W's in a sample of writing.
- Revise a sketchy informational piece by including the 5 W's, or making them more precise.

Teaching the Lesson

Step 1: Introducing the 5 W's

Begin by reviewing the 5 W's. Make sure students can recite the list, and that they understand what each one is. Then, look for the 5 W's in the brief examples that follow. The first example is done for you. Note that *every one* of the five may not be included in each example. As you go through the list, talk about what (if anything) is missing, and what else the writer *should* include.

1. In 1620, on November 9, a small ship called the Mayflower landed at Cape Cod, Massachusetts, with 101 emigrants aboard. They would establish a colony there, and come to be known as colonists.

    <u>__X__</u> Who   <u>__X__</u> What   <u>__X__</u> Where   <u>__X__</u> When   _____ Why

2. Winds are air currents. They are caused by temperature differences—which in turn are caused by the uneven heating of the Earth's surfaces. When a cold front and warm front collide, wind results. Doppler radar helps meteorologists determine the speed and direction of wind—which is invaluable in predicting when and where violent weather is likely to occur.

    _____ **Who**   _____ **What**   _____ **Where**   _____ **When**   _____ **Why**

3. The Great Wall of China is a man-made structure so large it is readily visible even from fairly high flying aircraft. Because of its size and the enormous effort required to build it, the Great Wall is considered one of the wonders of the modern world—even though it was built more than two thousand years ago, during the Qin Dynasty. The Great Wall is approximately four thousand miles long, and was built to keep invaders out of China. It was generally successful—though it did not stop Genghis Khan.

    _____ **Who**   _____ **What**   _____ **Where**   _____ **When**   _____ **Why**

Step 2: Making the Reading-Writing Connection

The Dangerous Book for Boys, by Conn Iggulden and Hal Iggulden, covers a wide range of subjects interesting not only to boys, but to readers in general. The 5 W's play a prominent role in the Igguldens' well-researched writing. How many of the five W's are included in this opening paragraph from a much longer (five-page) article in dinosaurs? Are any missing?

Sample

The term "dinosaur" means "terrible lizard," coined by a British scientist Richard Owen, in 1842. These reptiles roamed the earth for over a hundred and fifty million years, then mysteriously died out. They varied from fierce killers to giant plant eaters.

(Conn Iggulden and Hal Iggulden. *The Dangerous Book for Boys*. 2007. New York: HarperCollins. Page 30.)

In an opening paragraph, such as this one, an informational writer often gives readers a sample—just a *taste*—of *Who, What, Where,* or *When.* Then, the writer builds on that introductory sampling with more detail later. What, specifically, do you think these writers probably expanded on later in this same article? By the way, the introduction doesn't really address the *Why* question. *Why* does anyone trouble to study dinosaurs when they're now extinct? Two pages following the introduction, the writers offer this comment: "One of the most interesting things about studying dinosaurs is seeing how evolution took a different path before the slate was wiped clean . . ." (p. 31). Ah—there we go. Remember, in longer informational pieces, the 5 W's do not always come together, and do not always come in the first line!

Step 3: Involving Students as Evaluators

Ask students to review Samples A and B, specifically considering whether each writer includes all or some of the 5 W's, and whether each of the W's that are included is clearly and thoroughly addressed. Have students work with a partner, highlighting information that relates to one of the 5 W's and making marginal notes about any information noticeably missing.

Discussing Results

Most students should find Sample A stronger. Discuss differences between A and B, asking students what additional information the author of Sample B might have added to make the piece stronger. One possible revision of Sample B is provided.

Step 4: Modeling Revision

- If possible, provide students with factual information on dust mites.
- Share Sample C (*Whole Class Revision*) with students. Read it aloud.
- Talk about whether Sample C includes the 5 W's and addresses each one thoroughly. (Most students should say *no*.) Invite students to coach you through a class revision, identifying which of the 5 W's is missing, and adding new information to make the piece stronger.
- Base your revision on the information provided, and/or information gained through your own reading and investigation.
- When you finish, read your revision aloud. Did your additional information make the piece more complete? If you wish, compare your revision with ours.

Step 5: Revising with Partners

If possible, provide factual information on the Greenhouse Effect. Then, pass out copies of Sample D (*Revising with Partners*). Ask students to follow the basic steps you modeled with Sample C. *Working with partners,* they should:

- Read the passage aloud.
- Check to see how many of the 5 W's the writer has already included.
- Identify opportunities to add useful information.
- Revise by adding information, using data you provide or any personal research on the topic.
- Read the result aloud to hear the difference.
- (Optional) Verify any information added by further researching its authenticity.

Step 6: Sharing and Discussing Results

When students have finished, ask several pairs of students to share their revisions aloud. Who did the best job of covering the 5 W's? Who found additional information through research? (Feel free to share our suggested revision, keeping in mind that students' revisions need not match ours in any way.)

Next Steps

- The 5 W's are easy to spot in journalistic writing. Using any good newspaper for practice, look at the opening paragraph first—then at the article as a whole. The more your students practice looking for the 5 W's in the writing of others, the more they will be conscious of them in their own work.

- Use the 5 W's as a planning guide for a longer informational piece on any topic. Create a graphic in which *each* of the W's represents one column, and encourage students to fill each column with information from their research (the columns will *not* necessarily be equivalent in length). This graphic is a good indicator of whether the research is strong enough to support a thorough informational piece.

- Listen and look for the 5 W's in the literature you share aloud. Recommended:
  - *The Dangerous Book for Boys* by Conn Iggulden and Hal Iggulden. 2007. New York: HarperCollins.
  - *The Daring Book for Girls* by Andrea J. Buchanan and Mirian Peskowitz. 2007. New York: HarperCollins.
  - *Buzz: The Intimate Bond Between Humans and Insects* by Josie Glausiusz. 2004. San Francisco: Chronicle Books.
  - *Hidden Worlds: Looking Through a Scientist's Microscope* by Stephen Kramer. 2001. Boston: Houghton Mifflin.

- *For an additional challenge:* If you have a school newspaper, ask students to write journalistic articles that might be published in that paper. (It's good practice, even if they do not get published.) If your school does not put out a paper, consider having students write for another source. Look up "student publishing" online for a list.

Sample A

The shape of the pyramid has an almost mystical appeal to the human eye. The first pyramid ever built, the so-called Step Pyramid, was built over 4,600 years ago by an Egyptian king named Zoser. Though age has worn its ancient walls, it still rises today from the sands of Egypt. Pyramids are most closely associated with Egypt, yet modern versions do exist. Perhaps the most famous is the glass pyramid designed by American architect I. M. Pei. It forms the entrance to the Louvre Museum in Paris.

©2009. Allyn & Bacon, a division of Pearson Education. Developed by Vicki Spandel. All rights reserved.

Sample B

Avalanches occur routinely in mountainous regions throughout the world. They can be triggered in a number of ways. There are different kinds of avalanches, actually. Though most avalanches go unwitnessed by humans, they occur rather frequently, and can be extremely dangerous under the right circumstances. Consider how often people are visiting snow country these days with the growing popularity of winter sports such as snowboarding, skiing, snow shoeing, and snowmobiling. While there are precautions sports enthusiasts can take regarding avalanches, nothing can absolutely guarantee safety. No wonder avalanches are a growing concern.

©2009. Allyn & Bacon, a division of Pearson Education. Developed by Vicki Spandel. All rights reserved.

Suggested Revision of Sample B

on every continent, but they are most common in the Rocky Mountains, the Andes, the Himalayas, and the high mountain ranges of Europe.

Avalanches occur routinely ~~in mountainous regions~~

~~throughout the world.~~ They can be triggered in a number of

including rapid melting, weight from excessive snowfall, or sound.

ways. There are ~~different kinds of avalanches, actually~~

loose snow avalanches that form a widening V as they slide, and slab avalanches, in which a huge chunk of icy snow breaks free.

Though most avalanches go unwitnessed by humans, ~~they~~

scientists think there could be up to a million avalanches per year, with over 100,000 in North America alone! Because they often begin silently and without warning, all kinds

~~occur rather frequently, and~~ can be extremely dangerous

under the right circumstances. Consider how often people

are visiting snow country these days with the growing

popularity of winter sports such as snowboarding, skiing,

snow shoeing, and snowmobiling. ~~While there are~~

precautions Sports enthusiasts can take regarding

—they can stay out of so-called "back country," where no rescuers patrol, and they can use caution during warm periods of heavy melting. Still,

avalanches, nothing can absolutely guarantee safety. No

wonder avalanches are a growing concern.

*Information for this revision is based on *Avalanche* by Stephen Kramer, 1992. Minneapolis: Carolrhoda Books.

©2009. Allyn & Bacon, a division of Pearson Education. Developed by Vicki Spandel. All rights reserved.

Sample C: Whole Class Revision

Perhaps you have heard of dust mites. It's unlikely, however, that you have actually seen one. They are incredibly small. You would need to look under a microscope. That doesn't mean that you have not come into contact with a dust mite, however. They live in our homes, and are present virtually everywhere that humans are present. They can be obnoxious in a number of ways. At the same time, hard as it is to believe, dust mites can actually be helpful to humans. Whether they're helpful or not, though, many people would like to get rid of them. Unfortunately, it takes a little more than simple dusting to do that.

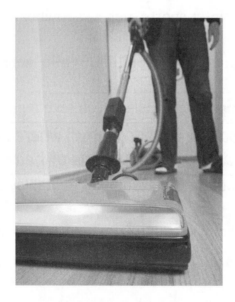

©2009. Allyn & Bacon, a division of Pearson Education. Developed by Vicki Spandel. All rights reserved.

Sample D: Revising with Partners

5 W's?

A greenhouse holds in heat. The Greenhouse Effect is like that, only bigger. The Greenhouse Effect keeps us warm on planet Earth. But lately, scientists say we are warming up too much, too fast. Fortunately, there are things we can do to reduce the impact. If we do nothing, there could be serious consequences.

©2009. Allyn & Bacon, a division of Pearson Education. Developed by Vicki Spandel. All rights reserved.

Suggested Revisions of C and D

Sample C: Whole Class Revision

Perhaps you have heard of dust mites. [*They're tiny insects that live on flakes of human skin.*] It's unlikely, however, that you have actually seen one. They are ~~incredibly small. You would~~ [*too small to see with the naked eye, but*] [*they look like big-eyed aliens from a space movie—complete with hairy legs.*] ~~need to look~~ under a microscope. ~~That doesn't mean that you have~~ [*carpets and furniture, and are particularly fond of hanging out in mattresses and pillows.*] ~~not come into contact with a dust mite, however.~~ They live in our ~~homes, and are present virtually everywhere that humans are~~ [*promoting asthma, hay fever, itchiness, and skin irritations.*] ~~present.~~ They can be obnoxious in a number of ways. At the same time, hard as it is to believe, dust mites can actually be helpful to [*if it weren't for these hungry bedfellows, we might be up to our knees in skin flakes and dandruff.*] humans; Whether they're helpful or not, though, many people would like to get rid of them. Unfortunately, it takes a little more than simple dusting to do that. Vacuuming helps, but the best cure seems to be providing dry surroundings. Dust mites don't drink; they take in water from the air. If the surroundings are too dry, they die. So—the lower the humidity, the fewer the mites.

*Information used in this revision is based on *Buzz: The Intimate Bond Between Humans and Insects* by Josie Glausiusz. 2004. San Francisco: Chronicle Books. Page 24.

©2009. Allyn & Bacon, a division of Pearson Education. Developed by Vicki Spandel. All rights reserved.

Sample D: Revising with Partners

A greenhouse holds in heat. [with glass, making plants grow.] The Greenhouse Effect [works the same way, except gases like carbon dioxide hold the heat in. Heat from the sun comes through the CO_2, but never escapes again.] ~~is like that, only bigger.~~ The Greenhouse Effect keeps us

warm on planet Earth. But lately, scientists say we are

warming up too much, too fast. Fortunately, there are things

we can do to reduce the impact. [such as driving less, or burning less coal and other fossil fuels.] If we do nothing, there

could be serious consequences. The polar ice caps could

melt, flooding parts of the Earth. It could become too

hot to farm as we do now. And some animals, like the

polar bear, could be endangered.

*Information for this revision is taken from two sources:

1. Bill Nye. *Bill Nye the Science Guy's Big Blast of Science.* 1993. New York: Addison-Wesley. Page 146.
2. John Roach. "Polar Bears Considered for U.S. Endangered List." For *National Geographic News.* February 10, 2006. Page 1.

©2009. Allyn & Bacon, a division of Pearson Education. Developed by Vicki Spandel. All rights reserved.

Commas in a Compound Sentence

Trait Connection: **Conventions**

Introduction (Share with students in your own words.)

Do you know what a compound sentence is? It's two smaller sentences hooked together with a little linking word called a *conjunction: and, but, or, for,* or *so*—as in these examples:

Jake hated snails, <u>and</u> he rarely ate them.

Jake and I hated snails, <u>but</u> they were Margaret's favorite thing.

We could have snails for dinner, <u>or</u> we could eat out.

Bill and Francine were relieved we ate out, <u>for</u> they were both snails.

Margaret was cooking, <u>so</u> we decided to fast.

Did you notice the punctuation that came right before those little coordinating words? If you said "Yes indeed, there was a comma in every single one of those sentences," you're in rare editing form today. By the way, in a top-notch compound sentence, you need both the comma, *and* the coordinating conjunction—the linking word. If you put in just the comma, it's a mistake called a *comma splice.* This term just means you tried to splice together two sentences using a comma, like this:

Jake hated snails, he rarely ate them.

Do you see what's missing from that sentence? The word *and.* Here's how we fix it:

and
Jake hated snails,˄he rarely ate them.

You already know how to insert a missing comma. Just tuck it inside a caret, like this:

Margaret was cooking˄so we decided to fast.

In the editing practice that follows, you'll insert four missing conjunctions (*and, but, for, or, so*) and four missing commas. Read the copy silently and aloud. You won't know which conjunction to use unless you pay attention to meaning. And

46

don't forget today's BIG editing hint: *The comma in a compound sentence always comes before the conjunction.*

Because *compound sentence* and *conjunction* are big, impressive terms, this sounds *a lot* harder than it is. It's a piece of cake. Get ready to roll your eyes at how simple this is.

Teaching the Lesson (General Guidelines for Teachers)

1. Share the examples above, or make up your own examples to practice using commas in a compound sentence.

2. Share the editing lesson on the following page. Students should read the passage silently and aloud, looking and listening for needed commas and missing coordinating conjunctions (*and, but, for, or, so*).

3. Ask them to edit individually first, then check with a partner.

4. When everyone is done, ask them to coach you as you edit the same copy.

5. When you finish, read your edited copy aloud; then compare it with our suggested text on page 49.

**Editing Goal: Fill in 4 missing coordinating conjunctions
and 4 missing commas.
Follow-Up: Check for correct use of commas and coordinating
conjunctions when editing your own work.**

Editing Practice

Insert missing conjunctions (*and, but, or, for, so*).
Insert missing commas before *and, but, or, for*, or *so*.

Molly wanted to go to the dance but Will wasn't having
any of it. "I could go by myself then, I could just stay
home and pout," Molly declared. She slammed the
door, it rattled on its wobbly hinges. She obviously
wasn't going to change her mind so Will finally caved
in. He went to the dance all right, he didn't have much
fun. Molly spent the whole night dancing with
someone else so Will sulked in the corner. Molly kept
asking him to dance, she couldn't coax him out of
hiding. Luckily, Will learned to dance before the next
party so Molly didn't have to get a new partner.

©2009. Allyn & Bacon, a division of Pearson Education. Developed by Vicki Spandel. All rights reserved.

Edited Copy

4 missing conjunctions (*and*, *but*, *or*, *so*) inserted
4 missing commas inserted before *and*, *but*, *or*, or *so*

Molly wanted to go to the dance, but Will wasn't

having any of it. "I could go by myself then, *or* I could

just stay home and pout," Molly declared. She slammed

the door, *and* it rattled on its wobbly hinges. She obviously

wasn't going to change her mind, so Will finally caved

in. He went to the dance all right, *but* he didn't have much

fun. Molly spent the whole night dancing with

someone else, so Will sulked in the corner. Molly kept

asking him to dance, *but* she couldn't coax him out of

hiding. Luckily, Will learned to dance before the next

party, so Molly didn't have to get a new partner.

©2009. Allyn & Bacon, a division of Pearson Education. Developed by Vicki Spandel. All rights reserved.

Revising a "How-to" Piece

Lesson 5

Trait Connection: **Ideas**

Introduction

Have you ever tried to follow a set of directions—how to cook something, how to put a toy or gadget together? If so, you know how important it is for writers of instructions to know what they are talking about. The best directions always seem to offer little tips that only an insider, someone who has been there and had the experience, would know. Insider knowledge gives a piece authenticity. It says to readers, "You can trust me. I've done this. I know what I'm talking about." Here's a little secret: If you want to write *really* good directions (the kind that won't make a frustrated reader give up on home-made chili and just order a pizza), try *doing* the thing first—even if you've done it once or twice before: bake the pie, play the game, train the dog. *Then*, with the experience fresh in your mind, *write*. You'll be amazed at the insight experience gives you.

Teacher's Sidebar . . .

The best "how-to" pieces, obviously, are written on subjects writers choose themselves. Only *they* are aware of which topics they know enough about to write with a sense of authenticity and insight. In this lesson, I have chosen topics with which students are likely to already have *some* experience, if only through reading or observation. The lesson is only a warm-up, however. Consider following up with practice writing "how-to" pieces on top-ics of students' *own choosing,* so they can put their personal expertise and insight to work.

Focus and Intent

This lesson is intended to help students:

- Understand the importance of clarity in a how-to piece.
- Distinguish between clear and unclear writing in how-to pieces.
- Revise a how-to piece to improve the clarity.

Teaching the Lesson

Step 1: Gaining Insight Through Experience

When it comes to writing an authentic how-to piece, nothing takes the place of firsthand experience—so create an experience for your students, involving a simple project. You (or a student) can do the modeling, while other students observe, comment, ask questions, and take notes. The idea is to become an expert at the task, through doing or watching. Choose something simple that you can *complete* in five minutes or less: e.g., making ice tea, potting a small plant, trimming and shaping an overgrown plant, entering phone numbers into a new cell phone, mending broken pottery with a hot glue gun, taking a photo, and so on. Talk as you model (or ask your student modeler to do this), commenting on anything that is difficult or surprising about the task. Ask student observers to:

1. Make careful notes on all the steps they observe, however tiny.

2. Look for "insights," the little things someone who has never done this task might not think of, such as—*When you trim an overgrown plant, make cuts close to the trunk or main stem of the plant.*

3. As a class, brainstorm those things someone reading your directions needs to know.

4. As a class, create a short "how-to" piece based on your experience.

Step 2: Making the Reading-Writing Connection

In a chapter called "Caring for Your Softball Glove," authors Andrea J. Buchanan and Miriam Peskowitz (*The Daring Book for Girls*) explain that however beautiful a new glove might be, it's a *broken in* glove that provides the best service. How did they know that, do you suppose? If you were reading this, and had just purchased a new glove, you might feel disappointed. But, no worries. They tell you just how to achieve that wonderful "broken in" feel, and how to know when you've gotten there:

Sample

Start by putting it on your hand, and with the other hand, toss a softball at it, over and over. Use your glove daily. Play catch with a parent or friend. Play toss-and-catch against a solid brick wall or a pitchback. Walk up and down the street tossing a ball into your glove. Your goal in breaking in the glove is to soften the leather and create a pocket for the ball. Your glove is properly broken in when you close the mitt and the thumb and pinkie come together and touch.

(From Andrea J. Buchanan and Miriam Peskowitz. *The Daring Book for Girls*. 2007. New York: HarperCollins. Page 49.)

What little details from this "how-to" paragraph tell us these writers are speaking from their own experience? Read the paragraph again and listen carefully. If you play softball yourself, is there anything *you* would add?

Step 3: Involving Students as Evaluators

Ask students to review Samples A and B, specifically considering whether each writer creates a clear "how-to" piece that suggests he or she is writing from experience and insight. Have students work with a partner, highlighting insightful information and making marginal notes about anything that is unclear.

Discussing Results

Most students should find Sample B stronger. Discuss differences between A and B, asking students what additional information the author of Sample A might have added to give the piece more clarity or a sense of authenticity. One possible revision of Sample A is provided.

Step 4: Modeling Revision

- As a class, brainstorm a short list of things your students already know from experience or from reading about how to build a campfire.

- Share Sample C (*Whole Class Revision*) with students. Read it aloud.

- Talk about whether Sample C is clear and offers insight based on experience (Most students should say *no*.) Invite students to coach you through a class revision, identifying a few insights based on what your students know about campfire building, and adding that information to make the piece stronger.

- When you finish, read your revision aloud. Did your additional information give the piece authenticity? If you wish, compare your revision with ours, remembering that it need not match ours in any way.

Step 5: Revising with Partners

With your students, brainstorm what they know about bowling. Then pass out copies of Sample D (*Revising with Partners)*. Ask students to follow the basic steps you modeled with Sample C. *Working with partners*, they should:

- Read the passage aloud.

- Check to see whether the writer offers insights based on experience or knowledge of the topic.

- Identify opportunities to add useful information.

- Revise by adding that information, using details from the brainstormed list or other personal knowledge.

- Read the result aloud to hear the difference.

Step 6: Sharing and Discussing Results

When students have finished, ask several pairs of students to share their revisions aloud. Did the teams' revisions give the new pieces authenticity? Who shared insider's information no other team thought of? (Feel free to share our suggested revision, keeping in mind that students' revisions need not match ours in any way.)

Next Steps

- Create "how-to" pieces based on personal experience or insider's knowledge, asking each student to choose a topic he or she knows well. Remind students that technical expertise is not essential to making this kind of writing work. Small topics—how to plant bulbs or train a puppy to heel or change a diaper—are just as effective as "how to build your own battery" or "how to build your own library of downloaded music" (though those are fine, too, for the student who knows how!).

■ This lesson is centered around the value of immediate experience in producing authentic writing. Use firsthand experience to create writing in other genres: e.g., personal narrative, description of a scene, character sketch, poetry, movie review, editorial, and so on.

■ Listen and look for authenticity based on experience in the literature you share aloud. Recommended:

● *The Dangerous Book for Boys* by Conn Iggulden and Hal Iggulden. 2007. New York: HarperCollins.

● *The Daring Book for Girls* by Andrea J. Buchanan and Mirian Peskowitz. 2007. New York: HarperCollins.

● *Hatchet: 20ᵗʰ Anniversary Edition* by Gary Paulsen. 2007. New York: Simon and Schuster. (Read the Introduction aloud to students; then share the many insightful sidebar notes Paulsen includes in this new edition that show how personal experience translates into believable fiction.)

● *American Boy's Handy Book: What to Do and How to Do It, Centennial Edition.* by Daniel Carter Beard. 1998. New York: David R. Godine.

● *American Girl's Handy Book: How to Amuse Yourself and Others*, by Lina Beard. 1994. New York: David R. Godine.

■ *For an additional challenge:* Ask students to demonstrate the value of experience with a topic of their choice by writing a "how-to" piece on that topic—then using experience to add the "little details" they didn't think of at first. Ask them not to change the original draft, but to write a new one, and to present both versions to the class so you can discuss the contrast.

Sample A

> Authentic detail? Insight?

Text messaging is a good way to send a message to a friend when you don't want to make an actual phone call. There are just a few things to keep in mind. One is to be careful entering your message so you don't make a mistake. People get very adept at this over time, but it can be tricky, so take your time. A great deal of text messaging involves abbreviations, which may not be totally familiar to some people, so this is another thing to watch out for. Courtesy is an important issue when sending a text message. Another issue—one not everyone thinks of—is safety.

On a scale of 1 to 10, what is the likelihood this writer has actually done any text messaging?

1_____5_____10

No way   Definitely

©2009. Allyn & Bacon, a division of Pearson Education. Developed by Vicki Spandel. All rights reserved.

Sample B

Authentic detail? Insight?

Most people listen to weather forecasts, but the truth is, you can do a lot to predict the weather yourself. Invest in a barometer. It will tell you whether barometric pressure is rising or falling. A rising barometer usually signals fair weather. A falling barometer signals incoming moisture. When violent weather is approaching, the barometer drops very rapidly. So does the temperature. A loss of more than eight degrees in a single hour often indicates an approaching storm. Weather tends to move in patterns. If most storm systems approach your area from the north or west, for instance, watch for increasing winds from those directions. Be especially watchful if you live in an area where warm and cold fronts collide; storms erupt along such lines. Remember that clouds are not all alike. High thin clouds rarely carry significant moisture and almost never signal coming turbulence. Thick cumulus clouds, on the other hand—the ones that appear to build right up out of the earth itself— nearly always portend stormy weather, and when they're accompanied by a falling barometer or rapid temperature drop, hail or sleet often follows. A colorful sunset often portends clear weather ahead, while a red sunrise may indicate a shift to stormier patterns. Similarly, a crystal clear night sky in the fall often precedes a hard frost.

On a scale of 1 to 10, what is the likelihood this writer has spent time learning how to predict weather?

1 _____ 5 _____ 10

No way   Definitely

©2009. Allyn & Bacon, a division of Pearson Education. Developed by Vicki Spandel. All rights reserved.

Suggested Revision of Sample A

Text messaging is a good way to send a message to a

> interrupt someone at an inconvenient time with a
> ringing phone. Texting is handy—and private, too.

friend when you don't want to ~~make an actual phone call,~~

There are just a few things to keep in mind. One is to be

careful entering your message so you don't make a mistake.

> fast with practice, using their fingers, thumbs—or
> a pen or pencil. But hitting the right keys rapidly

People get very ~~adept at this over time, but it~~ can be tricky,

so take your time. A great deal of text messaging involves

> Some, like BTW (by the way), LOL (laugh out loud), jk (just kidding), or
> sys (see you soon), are known to many people. But if you write ndpndnc
> (for independence), expect head scratching on the other end.

abbreviations. ~~which may not be totally familiar to some~~

~~people, so this is another thing to watch out for.~~ Courtesy is

> A good rule of thumb is not to text anything you wouldn't want intercepted,
> and of course, if someone sends you a message by mistake, let the person
> know—and then delete it. Also remember that a message doesn't always take
> the place of a personal call. Sometimes the recipient wants to hear your voice.

an important issue when sending a text message. Another

issue—one not everyone thinks of—is safety. Avoid text
messaging when driving or doing anything else that
demands full attention.

On a scale of 1 to 10, what is the likelihood that the person *who wrote this revision* has actually done any text messaging?

1 _____ 5 _____ 10

No way   Definitely

©2009. Allyn & Bacon, a division of Pearson Education. Developed by Vicki Spandel. All rights reserved.

Sample C: Whole Class Revision

Authentic
detail?
Insight?

Building a campfire is easier than you might think. You just need to remember a few things and take a few precautions. Start by choosing the right spot. You want your fire to burn well. You also want to make sure you and everyone around will be safe. Gather appropriate fuel to get the fire started, and put the materials together in such a way that the fire will keep burning. If you have matches, use them to start your fire. If you don't, you can use other methods. It is important to keep the fire going once it catches. How long you can keep it going depends on how much flammable material you have. When you do not need the fire anymore, be sure to put it out. This can be more difficult than it sounds. Check it before you leave the camping area to be sure it poses no danger to people or to the surroundings.

On a scale of 1 to 10, what is the likelihood that the writer regularly builds campfires?

1 _____ 5 _____ 10

No way   Definitely

©2009. Allyn & Bacon, a division of Pearson Education. Developed by Vicki Spandel. All rights reserved.

Sample D: Revising with Partners

Bowling seems to be enjoying a kind of revival these days—

for several reasons. It can be a lot of fun if you do it right.

First, it's important to wear the right clothing. You need the right

shoes also. Choose a good bowling ball; this is important. Take your

time and choose one that is right for you. When you are ready, hold

the ball with both hands, and walk forward until you're ready to

release it. Aim carefully! Roll the ball right down the alley toward

the pins. It might or might not go in a straight line. If you hit all the

pins on the first try, good for you! If you don't, don't worry because

you'll get another chance. Sometimes a ball goes into the gutter. The

best score you can get is 300 points in one game. But the most

important thing is to have fun.

> Authentic
> detail?
> Insight?

On a scale of 1 to 10, how likely do you think it is that this writer bowls regularly and knows the game well?

1 _____ 5 _____ 10

No way   Definitely

©2009. Allyn & Bacon, a division of Pearson Education. Developed by Vicki Spandel. All rights reserved.

Suggested Revisions of C and D

Sample C: Whole Class Revision

Building a campfire is easier than you might think. ~~You just need to remember a few~~

But the majority of forest fires are set by humans—many of them campers—so it's wise to

~~things and~~ take a few precautions. Start by choosing the right spot. You want your fire

So the "right" spot is one that is on bare earth, out of the wind, and away from trees, dry grass, or shrubs.

to burn well. You also want to make sure you and everyone around will be safe.

small dry twigs, branches the size of your thumb, and some dried moss

Gather ~~appropriate fuel~~ to get the fire started . ~~, and put the materials together in such~~

Build a kind of "tent" out of the materials, alternating moss and twigs, and allowing room for air. That way, the (*that's the easiest way*)

~~a way that~~ the fire will keep burning. If you have matches, ~~use them~~ to start your fire

—but they do need to be dry.   *have matches, use flint, or shine a light off a mirror or through glass to create enough heat to ignite your fire. Expect this to take a while!*

If you don't, ~~you can use other methods.~~ It is important to keep the fire going once it

Do this by gradually adding bigger and bigger branches—or logs. Twigs will only burn for seconds, but a five-inch diameter log may burn for an hour or even more, if it's dry.

catches. ~~How long you can keep it going depends on how much flammable material~~

~~you have.~~ When you do not need the fire anymore, be sure to put it out. This can be

Even if you don't see smoke or sparks, your fire may be smoldering, so cover it with earth or drench it in water.

more difficult than it sounds. Check it before you leave the camping area to be sure it

poses no danger to people or to the surroundings. **Don't just take a quick glance. Dig in the ground with a stick to make sure you cannot stir up any sparks or smoldering embers.**

On a scale of 1 to 10, what is the likelihood that *the reviser of this piece* has built campfires?

1 _____ 5 _____ 10

No way   Definitely

©2009. Allyn & Bacon, a division of Pearson Education. Developed by Vicki Spandel. All rights reserved.

Sample D: Revising with Partners

It is less expensive than many sports, is not weather-dependent, and is something even young children can do with minimal instruction.

Bowling seems to be enjoying a kind of revival these days—for several reasons. It

whether you get a high score or not!   loose, comfortable

can be a lot of fun if you do it right. First, it's important to wear the right clothing.

so you can glide across the floor and not trip when you release the ball!   as the right golf club or skiis   as   or tennis racket.

You need the right shoes also. Choose a good bowling ball; this is important. Take

a ball that is not too heavy to lift comfortably—with finger holes big enough so the ball slips from your hand easily.   about chest height

your time and choose one that is right for you. When you are ready, hold the ball with

four big steps toward the foul line. On the third step, swing the ball back, and on the fourth,

both hands, and walk forward until you're ready to release it. Aim carefully! Roll the

Some people curve the ball, hitting just right or left of the front pin.

center of the

ball right down the alley toward the pins. It might or might not go in a straight line. If

knock down all ten   that's a strike, and in bowling (unlike in baseball) strikes are good!   get a strike,

you hit all the pins on the first try, good for you! If you don't, don't worry because

and if you get all the remaining pins on your second try, it's called a spare.   Sorry, but you don't get any points for a gutter ball.

you'll get another chance. Sometimes a ball goes into the gutter. The best score you

You might bowl all your life and never hit the top score of   who cares?

can get is 300 points in one game. But, The most important thing is to have fun.

On a scale of 1 to 10, what is the likelihood that *the reviser of this piece* is familiar with the game of bowling?

1 _____ 5 _____ 10

No way   Definitely

©2009. Allyn & Bacon, a division of Pearson Education. Developed by Vicki Spandel. All rights reserved.

Run-On Sentences

Trait Connection: **Conventions**

Introduction (Share with students in your own words.)

In the last editing lesson, we looked at compound sentences: two smaller complete sentences joined by a comma and a little connecting word like *and, but, or, for,* or *so.* Take these two sentences:

It was raining and very late.

We took off for home at a dead run.

We can put these two sentences together to form a compound sentence like this one:

It was raining and very late, <u>so</u> we took off for home at a dead run.

That works just fine. What does NOT work is to run two smaller sentences together without any punctuation, like this:

It was raining and very late we took off for home at a dead run.

Read it again, slowly. See how confusing it is to have no pause between the sentences, and no linking word like *so?* This kind of sentence is called a *run-on.* The term describes what the sentence is doing. It is running on, out of control—and it is often hard to read such a sentence.

There are three ways to fix a run-on. They are all simple. You know one of them already: Just build a compound sentence, using a comma and a linking word such as *and, but, or, for*, or *so.* That's solution 1. You can also just make two short sentences, like this:

It was raining and very late. We took off for home at a dead run.

That's solution 2. Or, you can link the two little sentences using a semicolon. That makes one bigger sentence that would look like this:

It was raining and very late; we took off for home at a dead run.

Semicolons are great for linking sentences that are closely connected—like twins that are not identical, but are still closely related:

> When it came to plants, Jesse had a green thumb; when it came to pets, however, she had no skill at all.

See how those two sentences tell two sides of the same story? Jesse is good with plants—bad with pets. The semicolon —solution 3—tells us those ideas are related. Notice that there is no capital letter on the word *when* that follows the semicolon.
One way NOT to connect two sentences is with a comma all by itself:

> Brianna fell, she got up and kept running.

That kind of run-on is called a *comma splice*. It doesn't work because compared to semicolons or periods, commas don't have much power. They have enough to make us stop and breathe, but not enough to stop a sentence in its tracks. Here are four run-on sentences you can practice on, using one of the three editorial solutions we talked about: (1) make two sentences, (2) use a comma **and** a conjunction (*and, but, or, for, so*), or (3) use a semicolon. Try them all!

1. Juno's cat ate fourteen goldfish the next day he got a terrible stomach ache.

2. Eduardo took a class in karate, we were delighted when he shared some lessons with us.

3. Our teacher assigned ten chapters out of the history textbook we finished them all before dinnertime.

4. Amazingly, Mindy just had her thirtieth birthday she actually looks no more than twenty.

Teaching the Lesson (General Guidelines for Teachers)

1. Share the examples above, or make up your own examples to practice correcting run-on sentences using a semicolon or a comma and coordinating conjunction (*and, but, or, for, so*).

2. Make sure that students understand it is all right to make the correction either way.

3. Share the editing lesson on the following page. Students should read the passage silently and aloud, looking and listening for run-on sentences (sometimes called *comma splices* when a comma is used to split the sentences). They should correct each one by inserting a semicolon or a comma *and* coordinating conjunction (*and, but, or, for, so*). They should find five run-on sentences (three without *any* punctuation and two in which independent clauses, or sentences, are divided only by a comma).

4. Ask them to edit individually first, then check with a partner.

5. When everyone is done, ask them to coach you as you edit the same copy.

6. When you finish, read your edited copy aloud, pausing to explain each correction as necessary; then compare it with our suggested text on page 65.

7. If students have difficulty with this lesson, repeat the four practice sentences, and add a few of your own. Then repeat the lesson, asking students to work with a different partner.

8. *Note:* Use as much or as little grammatical terminology in this lesson as you wish. What is important is for students to know how to link two smaller sentences together to make a larger sentence.

Editing Goal: Correct 5 run-ons.
Follow-Up: Check for run-ons in your own work, and correct them using one of the strategies described in this lesson.

Editing Practice

Correct 5 run-ons.
You can:
- **Make 2 sentences**
- **Use a comma <u>and</u> conjunction** (*and, but, or, for, so*)
- **Use a semicolon (;)**

Joaquin had painting in his blood he just could not seem to stop himself from picking up a brush. He was always painting something—a portrait of a friend, a landscape, or his dog leaping through the air. One day he got inspired, he painted a giant mural around the perimeter of his room. Joaquin's mother was not pleased she was furious, in fact. She ordered him to repaint the entire room in its original shade of yellow, Joaquin could not bring himself to do it. It was just as well. When a friend saw the mural, he offered to give Joaquin free art lessons he said he had never seen so much talent in someone only ten years old.

©2009. Allyn & Bacon, a division of Pearson Education. Developed by Vicki Spandel. All rights reserved.

Edited Copy

5 run-ons corrected

Joaquin had painting in his blood, he just could not seem to

stop himself from picking up a brush. He was always

painting something—a portrait of a friend, a landscape, or

his dog leaping through the air. One day he got inspired, *and* he

painted a giant mural around the perimeter of his room.

Joaquin's mother was not pleased, she was furious, in fact.

She ordered him to repaint the entire room in its original

shade of yellow, *but* Joaquin could not bring himself to do it. It

was just as well. When a friend saw the mural, he offered to

give Joaquin free art lessons. He said he had never seen so

much talent in someone only ten years old.

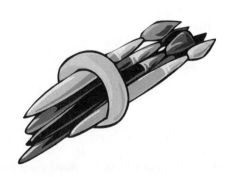

©2009. Allyn & Bacon, a division of Pearson Education. Developed by Vicki Spandel. All rights reserved.

Revising for Coherence

Trait Connection: **Organization**

Introduction

Did you ever start out talking about one thing, and wind up talking about something else altogether? Most people do this occasionally. When we're speaking, it isn't so serious to get sidetracked because we can say something like, "Let's see—what were we talking about? Oh, right—*rutabagas!*" But in writing, it's different. As a writer, you're not there (usually) to explain yourself. The reader has to figure out where you're going and why you chose to take a particular turn in the road. Sometimes, a writer has a good reason for making such a turn. But often, he or she is simply distracted. Forgetting your main topic, even for a few seconds, is like taking your eyes off the road to watch the cows grazing in the nearby field. Before you know it, you're up to your eyeballs in cows, wondering how you got there. This lesson is about *coherence*—keeping your eyes on the "road," which is to say, your main topic.

Teacher's Sidebar . . .

Sometimes a writer appears to be sidetracked, but the new sub-topic *is* actually related to the topic. For example, a student might be writing about dinosaurs and suddenly begin writing about eagles. Birds are descendents of dinosaurs, but if the writer does not make that connection clear, some readers will find the apparent shift jarring, as well as confusing. From the writer's point of view, it is good to keep two guidelines in mind: (1) take side trips *only* when you have an important point to make, and (2) make the connection crystal clear for the reader.

Focus and Intent

This lesson is intended to help students:

- Understand the concept of coherence.
- Recognize when a writer is going off track.
- Revise an incoherent piece to restore coherence.

Teaching the Lesson

Step 1: Introducing the Concept of Coherence

Coherence lends continuity (the sense of a continuous, uninterrupted flow) to writing. In a coherent piece, the writer has a clear vision. He or she has a point to make or a story to tell, and sticks with it, taking care not to wander. Related subtopics may be brought in, but the writer is careful to show how they connect to the main theme. In the following two examples, the writer is sometimes coherent, sometimes not. Ask students to identify *each moment* when the writer goes off on a sidetrack. Is the new topic *potentially* related? If so, how could the writer make the connection clear?

1. The average child watches hundreds of hours of television each week. While we often think of cartoons as an innocent form of entertainment, the truth is, many cartoons are extremely violent. Though no real blood is shed, cartoon characters are injured, flattened by vehicles, or hurled off cliffs. Many adults actually enjoy violence as a part of their entertainment.

2. Some middle schools and high schools now have dress code rules banning the wearing of certain jewelry, such as large bracelets, pendants, or oversized earrings. Because jewelry is so expensive these days, not all students can afford it. Certainly, some jewelry can be distracting, both to the wearer and to others. Actually, the wearing of jewelry is part of numerous cultural traditions throughout the world.

Step 2: Making the Reading-Writing Connection

In a book called *The Schwa Was Here*, the narrator Anthony tells us just how hard it is to keep his friend Calvin (aka "the Schwa") in his mind. Calvin simply fades from memory—like a history lesson. Notice what a hard time Anthony has thinking about the Schwa even while he is talking about him:

Sample

He was like trying to remember Lewis and Clark, and Manifest Destiny—both of which I had to do oral reports on, and if you've ever had to do an oral report, you probably know how they make you dress up like whoever you're doing the report on, but how was I supposed to dress up like Manifest Destiny? I got marked down because I wore jeans and a T-shirt . . .

(Neal Shusterman. *The Schwa Was Here*. 2004. New York: Puffin Books. Page 162.)

What does this have to do with Calvin, the Schwa, again? Uh—nothing. It makes for some pretty funny reading in this example, where Anthony is *showing* us how hard it is to focus on the Schwa, even for a *few seconds*, even when he is *trying* to talk about him. But this is a comic moment. In a serious informational essay or persuasive argument, you do *not* want to wander from your main point.

Step 3: Involving Students as Evaluators

Ask students to review Samples A and B, specifically considering whether each writer creates a coherent piece that stays on track. Have students work with a partner, highlighting any text that shows the writer wandering off track and discussing whether or not these off-track points are connected to the writer's main topic.

Discussing Results

Most students should find Sample A stronger. Discuss differences between A and B, asking students where Writer B goes off track, and whether the seemingly unrelated points could be connected, or should just be deleted. Either option is acceptable. One possible revision of Sample B is provided.

Step 4: Modeling Revision

- Share Sample C (*Whole Class Revision*) with students. Read it aloud.

- Talk about whether Sample C is coherent. (Most students should say *no*.) Invite students to coach you through a class revision, identifying those places where the writer wanders, and deciding whether to forge a connection to the main point—or simply delete the unrelated material. (There is no "right" answer to this, and your approach to revision is up to you.)

- When you finish, read your revision aloud. Did your changes give the piece more coherence? If you wish, compare your revision with ours, remembering that it need not match ours in any way.

Step 5: Revising with Partners

Pass out copies of Sample D (*Revising with Partners*). Ask students to follow the basic steps you modeled with Sample C. *Working with partners,* they should:

- Read the passage aloud.

- Notice whether and when the writer wanders from the main topic.

- Identify opportunities to either make stronger connections or delete unrelated material.

- Revise by either strengthening connections or deleting those parts of the text that wander.

- Read the result aloud to hear the difference.

Step 6: Sharing and Discussing Results

When students have finished, ask several pairs of students to share their revisions aloud. Did teams' revisions increase coherence? Which teams deleted unrelated material, and which found a way to connect them to the writer's main point? Which form of revision is easier? (Feel free to share our suggested revision, keeping in mind that students' revisions need not match ours in any way.)

Next Steps

■ Neal Schusterman's introduction to Chapter 16 of *The Schwa Was Here* (from which our Reading-Writing Connection example was taken) is very funny, and you may wish to share a larger portion aloud with your students. It is also fun to imitate. This free-writing, free-thinking kind of approach is actually a very good way for writers to identify topics that are of personal importance to them. Ask students to write without making an effort to stick with *any* topic, just going wherever their minds lead them. Wandering on purpose can actually create a mental contrast that makes achieving coherence easier.

■ When students meet in response groups, ask them to listen for any moments when writers wander, and to note those occasions on a 3×5 card. All cards should later be given to the writers. If a given moment is only noted on *one* card, it is likely the *listener* wasn't paying attention! But if it shows up on three cards, the writer probably did wander—or the connection was unclear.

■ Listen and look for coherence (or lack of it) in the literature you share aloud. Recommended (for examples of coherent informational writing):

• *Blizzard* by Jim Murphy. 2000. New York: Scholastic.

• *The Story of Salt* by Mark Kurlansky. 2006. New York: G. P. Putnam's Sons.

• *Tracking Trash: Flotsam, Jetsam, and the Science of Ocean Motion* by Loree Griffin Burns. 2007. Boston: Houghton Mifflin.

■ *For an additional challenge:* Ask students to write a coherent summary of any book on the recommended list—or any other book of their choice. The summary should capture all key elements of the book within a half page or less (about 250 words). Imagine that the summary will be printed in a newsletter featuring books recommended by a local bookstore.

Sample A

Coherent?
Wandering?

When humans set out to build a house, they need to

think carefully about the overall design—and most of the

time, they do not know what the final product will look

like. Every human's house is potentially unique. There is no

one design that fits all. With animal species, it is altogether

different. Each spider knows, from instinct, precisely how

to design a web. Each bird knows just how to build a nest—

and what is more, an eagle's nest resembles that of other

eagles, and a robin's nest resembles that of other robins.

Coyotes' dens, beavers' dams, or wasps' nests all fit a

pattern peculiar to that species. There is no "ranch style"

wasp nest, or "Victorian" beaver dam.

©2009. Allyn & Bacon, a division of Pearson Education. Developed by Vicki Spandel. All rights reserved.

Sample B

How is an ant hill formed, anyway? Simple. The ants simply deposit the soil that comes from burrowing their tunnels right on top—and presto, they have a hill. Of course, not every hill you see in a field is an ant hill; some are formed in other ways. The hill itself may also be excavated, of course, so the ant village grows ever larger.

One of the most interesting things about ants is that they are very difficult to disturb. This is definitely not true of other insects, such as wasps. It is not true of all animals, either. It is literally possible to slice right into an ant colony to see what is happening inside, and the ants will go right on with their business as if nothing unusual were happening at all. They do eventually repair the damage caused by the intrusion, but they don't get all flustered right at the moment. This makes ants extremely easy to observe.

©2009. Allyn & Bacon, a division of Pearson Education. Developed by Vicki Spandel. All rights reserved.

Suggested Revision of Sample B

How is an ant hill formed, anyway? Simple. The ants
simply deposit the soil that comes from burrowing their
tunnels right on top—and presto, they have a hill. ~~Of
course, not every hill you see in a field is an ant hill; some
are formed in other ways.~~ The hill itself may also be
excavated, of course, so the ant village grows ever larger.

One of the most interesting things about ants is that
they are very difficult to disturb. This is definitely not true
(but perhaps ants just aren't as nervous as wasps.)
of other insects, such as wasps. ~~It is not true of all animals
either.~~ It is literally possible to slice right into an ant colony
to see what is happening inside, and the ants will go right
on with their business as if nothing unusual were happening
at all. They do eventually repair the damage caused by the
intrusion, but they don't get all flustered right at the
moment. This makes ants extremely easy to observe,
especially in comparison to wasps!

©2009. Allyn & Bacon, a division of Pearson Education. Developed by Vicki Spandel. All rights reserved.

Sample C: Whole Class Revision

Coherent?
Wandering?

Evolution is a slow, orderly process of change, through which plant and animal species adapt to changes in the world—such as changes in climate. An increase in the crime rate of cities would be another example of change. Animals that adapt thrive.

Animals don't plan this change. It just happens. You see this with people, too. People are all different—and that makes us interesting. Some people are born with longer legs than others, for example. If the differences that pop up help a species to survive, they will be passed on to the offspring. For example, if tortoises with harder shells resist predators, then hard-shelled tortoises are more likely to thrive. If giraffes with longer necks can reach better food from the trees, the long-necked giraffes will have more offspring.

©2009. Allyn & Bacon, a division of Pearson Education. Developed by Vicki Spandel. All rights reserved.

Sample D: Revising with Partners

Coherent?
Wandering?

Of all the different kinds of debris in the world, one of the most harmful is plastic. Plastic does not dissolve—and it is impossible to digest. In recent years, plastic has become increasingly popular, especially in toy manufacturing. It is light and durable. It's very colorful, too! Over time, plastic trash like toys, bottle caps, or sports equipment, may be broken into smaller bits by the effects of surf or weather. It is never absorbed into the earth, however. It actually becomes even more dangerous when broken apart because animals and birds mistake the small pieces of plastic for food. They eat it—then die. Scientists believe it is very important for us to think about the way we manufacture and use plastics. No doubt we'll discover even more uses for this versatile product in the future!

©2009. Allyn & Bacon, a division of Pearson Education. Developed by Vicki Spandel. All rights reserved.

Suggested Revisions of C and D

Sample C: Whole Class Revision

Evolution is a slow, orderly process of change, through which plant and animal species adapt to changes in the world—such as changes in climate. ~~An increase in the crime rate of cities would be another example of change.~~ Animals that adapt thrive.

Animals don't plan this change. It just happens. ~~You see this with people, too. People are all different—and that makes us interesting. Some people are born with longer legs than others, for example.~~ If the differences that pop up help a species to survive, they will be passed on to the offspring. For example, if tortoises with harder shells resist predators, then hard-shelled tortoises are more likely to thrive. If giraffes with longer necks can reach better food from the trees, the long-necked giraffes will have more offspring.

©2009. Allyn & Bacon, a division of Pearson Education. Developed by Vicki Spandel. All rights reserved.

Sample D: Revising with Partners

Of all the different kinds of debris in the world, one of

the most harmful is plastic. Plastic does not dissolve—

and it is impossible to digest. In recent years, plastic has

become increasingly popular, especially in toy

(Every year we make more—and throw more away.)

manufacturing. ~~It is light and durable. It's very colorful~~

~~too.~~ Over time, plastic trash like toys, bottle caps, or

sports equipment, may be broken into smaller bits by the

effects of surf or weather. It is never absorbed into the

earth, however. It actually becomes even more dangerous

when broken apart because animals and birds mistake the

small pieces of plastic for food. They eat it—then die.

Scientists believe it is very important for us to think about

(In the meantime, we must be very careful how we dispose of it.)

the way we manufacture and use plastics. ~~No doubt we'll~~

~~discover even more uses for this versatile product in the~~

~~future.~~

©2009. Allyn & Bacon, a division of Pearson Education. Developed by Vicki Spandel. All rights reserved.

Putting It Together
(Editing Lessons 2, 4, and 6)

Trait Connection: **Conventions**

Introduction (Share with students in your own words.)

In this lesson, you will have a chance to put skills from three editing lessons together. You will

- Edit to insert commas in a series:

  We finished our homework, did the dishes, and went to bed.

- Edit to insert commas in compound sentences (before *and, but, or, for*, or *so*):

  The wind was blowing nearly 70 miles an hour, <u>so</u> we gave up walking the beach.

- Edit run-ons:

  Roger was captain of the football team he really preferred basketball, however.

  by any of three methods:

  1. Make two sentences:

     Roger was captain of the football team. He really preferred basketball, however.

  2. Make a compound sentence, using *and, but, or, for*, or *so*, and a comma:

     Roger was captain of the football team, <u>but</u> he really preferred basketball. (Delete *however* with this version.)

  3. Insert a semicolon:

     Roger was captain of the football team; he really preferred basketball, however.

Teaching the Lesson (General Guidelines for Teachers)

1. Begin by reviewing the concepts: a *series*, a *compound sentence*, a *run-on*. Make sure all three are clear in students' minds.

2. Review the little linking words (conjunctions) used to link the two parts of a compound sentence: *and, but, or, for, so.* Remind students that in a compound sentence, the comma comes *before* the linking word.

3. Review the three ways to edit a run-on sentence: (1) Make two sentences, (2) create a compound sentence using a linking word and a comma, or (3) insert a semicolon. Practice all three, using the example above and/or one of your own.

4. Answer any questions students may have. Encourage them to review Lessons 2, 4, and 6—and even to refer to these as they work on Lesson 8.

5. Share the editing lesson on the following page. Students should read the passage aloud, looking *and listening* for things they wish to change.

6. Ask them to work individually first, then check with a partner.

7. When everyone is done, ask them to coach you as you edit the same copy, making any changes you and they decide are important.

8. When you finish, compare your edited copy to the one on page 80.

9. *Note:* The students' way of editing the two run-ons may or may not match ours; what is important is that they edit each run-on, using *any acceptable method.*

Editing Goals:
Insert missing commas in 2 series.
Insert missing commas in 2 compound sentences.
Edit 2 run-ons in any acceptable way.

Editing Practice

Insert missing commas in a series.
Insert missing commas in compound sentences.
Edit run-ons.

Aiden raced home changed into his uniform grabbed his soccer ball and bolted out the door. His friends Charlie Matt and José were already waiting for him across the street. He kicked the soccer ball in their direction but his timing was so far off that he almost hit a car coming down the road. "Watch it!" Charlie yelled, grabbing the ball from the gutter. Laughing, Aiden shot across the road the three friends headed off for the soccer field. As they approached the field, Aiden could see the coach checking his watch and he knew they were running late. They picked up the pace. The coach tried hard to look stern the boys could see a smile spreading across his face.

©2009. Allyn & Bacon, a division of Pearson Education. Developed by Vicki Spandel. All rights reserved.

Edited Copy

Commas inserted in 2 series
Commas inserted in 2 compound sentences
2 run-ons corrected

Aiden raced home, changed into his uniform, grabbed his

soccer ball, and bolted out the door. His friends Charlie,

Matt, and José were already waiting for him across the

street. He kicked the soccer ball in their direction, but his

timing was so far off that he almost hit a car coming down

the road. "Watch it!" Charlie yelled, grabbing the ball from

the gutter. Laughing, Aiden shot across the road, *and* the three

friends headed off for the soccer field. As they approached

the field, Aiden could see the coach checking his watch,

and he knew they were running late. They picked up the

pace. The coach tried hard to look stern, *but* the boys could see

a smile spreading across his face.

©2009. Allyn & Bacon, a division of Pearson Education. Developed by Vicki Spandel. All rights reserved.

Revising by Chunking

Trait Connection: **Organization**

Introduction

Chunking is a technique some writers use to plan their writing. Wait a minute, though . . . if chunking is part of *planning*, why would we already be *revising?* Good question. Revision doesn't just happen toward the end of the writing process. Re-vision is re-thinking. Rethinking the overall design of your writing early on can make later revision much simpler. Here's why. Think of writing as building a house. It doesn't make sense to talk about the smaller details of walls, carpeting, and windows until you know how large a house will be, how many rooms it will have, and whether it will be one or two stories high. Writing is like that. Once you have the larger concept in your mind—the major topics you will cover—it's easier to zero in on smaller issues, such as writing a good lead or using sensory details to liven up description. So, first things first. Let's do some chunking—uh, *designing*.

Teacher's Sidebar . . .

Chunking is a little different from outlining in that it's nonlinear. It's more like putting a puzzle together. Instead of just writing or typing everything on one sheet of paper, encourage students to write descriptions of various chunks on 5×7 cards or half sheets of paper that they can move around freely. This allows them to examine several designs within a matter of seconds. It also gives a writer enormous flexibility to add or delete things during any part of the writing process. As part of this lesson, we'll ask students to cut "chunks" apart so that they can do this kind of manipulation—or to write on 3×5 cards of their own. Please keep in mind that there is never one "right" answer to design. The objective is to create a smooth, easy-to-follow flow of ideas that guides the reader.

Focus and Intent

This lesson is intended to help students:

- Understand the concept of chunking.
- Recognize various design possibilities.
- Revise by coming up with one possibility that creates a smooth flow.

Teaching the Lesson

Step 1: Going for the "Top 5" Chunks

If you were writing something long, like a textbook, you might have *many* chunks of information—say, 100 or more. For this warm-up, we'll ask you to keep the number of chunks to just *five*. Choose a topic—something your students are currently studying. Then follow these steps:

Step 1

Brainstorm eight important things you know, as a class, about this topic (feel free to contribute from your own knowledge). Post the list where everyone can see it.

Step 2

Whittle your list of eight down to the "Top 5." All eight may be important—but imagine your space is limited and you cannot cover everything. (Eliminating what is less than essential is a vital organizational skill in writing—just as in cleaning closets.)

Step 3

Put the remaining five in an order that makes sense—by asking these questions: What's the simplest, most basic information? (Put that first.) What do readers need to know before they can understand other things? (Also put that up front.) Which chunks are really big—or answer questions raised early on? (Put those in the middle.) What do I want to leave readers thinking about? (Put that last.)

Step 2: Making the Reading-Writing Connection

(*Note:* For this part of the lesson, divide students into teams of two or three. Give each team <u>six</u> 3×5 cards on which they can write subtopics.)

How do you feel about cockroaches? David George Gordon, biologist and bug lover, found them so fascinating that he wrote a whole book about them—a sort of tribute. That book has numerous subtopics. Following are just six of them. Write each one on a 3×5 card. (You only need to *write* the <u>underlined part</u>, not the whole description.) Then put them into an order you think Gordon might have used in his book.

1. <u>Cockroaches as pets</u>. This chunk tells of cockroach "tricks," places to purchase cockroaches, how to trap your own pet cockroach, and how to house and feed your pet.

2. <u>Controlling cockroaches</u>. This chunk includes remedies used throughout history (including renting hedgehogs!): poison, traps, heat, dehydration, geckos, and the dreaded "killer fungi."

3. <u>Uses for cockroaches</u>. Goodness. Are cockroaches *useful?* This chunk tells us they are, looking at the role cockroaches play in medical research, as a source of animal food, and even in human cuisine. Yummmmm.

4. <u>The perils of being a cockroach</u>. It isn't easy, you know. The list of cockroach enemies includes cats, rodents, reptiles, birds, mammals, man (of course!), and sometimes their own kind. Yikes. Cannibalism!

5. <u>The history of cockroaches</u>. This chunk describes how long cockroaches have been on earth, looks at cockroach fossils, cockroach ancestors—and the means by which cockroaches have spread, via ships and planes, to every corner of civilization—even into space!

6. <u>What is a cockroach</u>? You might think you know all about them—but there's a lot to know. This chunk defines and describes cockroaches. It covers anatomy, statistics on size, and kinds of cockroaches, and includes numerous labeled illustrations.

These subtopics are taken from the book *The Compleat Cockroach* by David George Gordon (1996. Berkeley, CA: Ten Speed Press). Gordon's order was as follows:

1. What is a cockroach? (number 6 on our list)

2. History of cockroaches (5 on our list)

3. Uses for cockroaches (3 on our list)

4. Perils of being a cockroach (4 on our list)

5. Cockroaches as pets (1 on our list)

6. Controlling cockroaches (2 on our list)

Do you see the logic in Gordon's organization? Was your design different?

Step 3: Involving Students as Evaluators

Ask students to review Samples A and B, specifically considering whether each writer has chunked a proposed report into an order that makes sense. Have students work with a partner, actually cutting the proposed designs into chunks and playing with the order to test the writer's original.

Discussing Results

Most students should find Sample A stronger. It is logical and simple. Discuss differences between A and B, asking students what Writer B might have done differently, and how they would have ordered these chunks of information. One possible revision of Sample B is provided.

Step 4: Modeling Revision

- Share Sample C (*Whole Class Revision*) with students. Read it aloud.

- Talk about whether the writer of Sample C has chunked information in a way that is both inviting and easy to follow. (Most students should say *no*.) Invite students to coach you through a class revision, reorganizing chunks—and possibly deleting something. (There is no "right" answer to this, and your organizational design is up to you. Just be sure you can talk through reasons for your changes.)

- When you finish, review the new design by reading through the chunks aloud. Is the organizational structure inviting? Is it easy to follow? If you wish, compare your revision with ours, remembering that many organizational designs are possible, and yours need not match ours.

Step 5: Revising with Partners

Pass out copies of Sample D (*Revising with Partners*). Ask students to follow the basic steps you modeled with Sample C. *Working with partners,* they should:

- Read the current design aloud.

- Cut the chunks apart so that they can play with the order. (They are numbered, so the original order is simple to restore.)

- Reorganize information in a way that makes sense—and, if desired, delete one or more chunks. (Also feel free to add something new.)

- Read the result aloud to hear the difference, making sure they can talk through reasons behind their new organizational structure.

Step 6: Sharing and Discussing Results

When students have finished, ask several pairs of students to share their revisions aloud. Did teams' revisions improve the organizational design? How many different designs did students, as a class, come up with? Which teams deleted one or more chunks? (Feel free to share our suggested revision, keeping in mind that students' revisions need not match ours in any way.)

Next Steps

- Chunking can be used for almost any piece of writing, from a short paragraph to a long textbook (in which chunks would be chapters). You can explore a writer's thinking at work by making your own chunk puzzles and solving them. Make a copy first. Then cut a paragraph into sentence strips and re-order them. Or, cut a longer piece into paragraphs. For a really long piece, such as a history book, try slicing up the table of contents and see if you can restore it to its original version—or even come up with something better!

- When students meet in response groups, ask writers to put one chunk (usually one subtopic or one paragraph) on 3×5 cards (the same for everyone) and pass these out before reading. As they're reading, they need to skip over that chunk totally—and see if listeners can hear where it should go.

■ Listen and look for effective design in the literature you share aloud. Some writers not only have a much stronger sense of organizational design than others, but also use subtitles creatively to make their design visible and obvious to readers (an example of presentation supporting organization). Recommended:

● *The Compleat Cockroach* by David George Gordon. 1996. Berkeley, CA: Ten Speed Press.

● *Bill Nye the Science Guy's Big Blast of Science* by Bill Nye. 1993. New York: Addison Wesley.

● *Pocket Babies and Other Amazing Marsupials* by Sneed B. Collard III. 2007. Plain City, OH: Darby Creek Publishing.

■ *For an additional challenge:* Invite students to use the technique of chunking in designing a research piece. Once they come up with the original design, they should turn each "chunk" into a **file folder**, and label it appropriately. Into each folder they can put the facts, quotations, illustrations, notes, and bibliographic entries relating to that chunk—and that chunk *only*. As their research continues, they have freedom to divide any chunk into two if it grows really big—or to drop it if they can't find information to fill the folder. Notes and quotations can be taped or glued to the inside of the file folder, creating a helpful visual display when the folder is opened. When it's time to draft the report, students can line up their folders, and write from one at a time. Martha Stewart, eat your heart out.

Sample A

Report on Pigs

Good design? Anything out of order?

1. <u>Anatomy of the pig</u>: What pigs look like, and a labeled sketch.

2. <u>Kinds of pigs</u>: A quick review of different breeds, what they look like, and how they're used: food, pets, truffle hunting.

3. <u>Pig brains</u>: The intelligence of pigs—what they can do and how they blow away the competition—e.g., dogs or cats.

4. <u>Pigs around the world</u>: Which countries have the largest pig populations—and why.

5. <u>Wild pigs</u>: Where they live, how they differ from domestic pigs, whether they're dangerous, whether you can hunt them.

6. <u>A pig of your own</u>: If you want to raise pigs—for food or as pets—what's involved? How hard is it? Do you have the right facilities—and the right *personality?*

- Would you drop any of these chunks (subtopics)? If so, which ones? Would you add anything new?
- Would you reorder anything? If so, how?

©2009. Allyn & Bacon, a division of Pearson Education. Developed by Vicki Spandel. All rights reserved.

Sample B

Good design? Anything out of order?

Avalanches

1. <u>Safety</u>: What to do if you are ever caught in an avalanche.

2. <u>Snow sports</u>: A quick review of different types of popular snow sports.

3. <u>Rescuing skiers</u>: How teams work to rescue skiers and other winter sports enthusiasts trapped by avalanches.

4. <u>Most likely locations</u>: Where avalanches occur, and how to avoid dangerous spots.

5. <u>Personal story</u>: An exciting, dramatic firsthand account of being in an avalanche.

6. <u>Forecasting</u>: What triggers an avalanche, and whether there is any way to predict them.

7. <u>What is an avalanche</u>? Definitions, descriptions, and photos of different types of avalanches.

8. <u>Tips on skiing</u>: Tips for skiing well and avoiding injuries.

- **Would you drop any of these chunks (subtopics)? If so, which ones?**
- **Would you reorder anything? If so, how?**
- **Would you add any new topics? If so, what?**

©2009. Allyn & Bacon, a division of Pearson Education. Developed by Vicki Spandel. All rights reserved.

Suggested Revision of Sample B

Avalanches

1. <u>Personal story</u>: An exciting, dramatic firsthand account of being in an avalanche. *(Formerly #5—This could be a good opener. It will hook readers.)*

2. <u>What is an avalanche</u>? Definitions, descriptions, and photos of different types of avalanches. *(Formerly #7—The basics.)*

3. <u>Most likely locations</u>: Where avalanches occur, and how to avoid dangerous spots. *(Formerly #4—An important question—still part of the basics.)*

4. <u>Rescuing skiers</u>: How teams work to rescue skiers and other winter sports enthusiasts trapped by avalanches. *(Formerly #3—A big and important topic—good for the middle.)*

5. <u>Safety</u>: What to do if you are ever caught in an avalanche. *(Formerly #1—Connected directly to Chunk 4.)*

6. <u>Forecasting</u>: What triggers an avalanche, and whether there is any way to predict them. *(Formerly #6—A good last thought: Can we know about them ahead of time? Or at least figure out what causes them?)*

Note
Chunks on snow sports (#2) and tips on skiing (#8) have been cut. Just because it has to do with snow does not mean it's related to avalanches! We did not add any new topics—but maybe you did.

©2009. Allyn & Bacon, a division of Pearson Education. Developed by Vicki Spandel. All rights reserved.

Sample C: Whole Class Revision

Roller Skating

Good design? Anything out of order?

1. Falling: Tips for falling properly so you can minimize injury.

2. Other equipment: An overview of other equipment you will need, including a helmet and knee pads.

3. Choosing skates: A guide to choosing roller skates that are comfortable, functional, and durable.

4. History: When the sport of roller skating began, how it has changed since the 1700s.

5. Ice skating: How it's like roller skating, how it's different.

6. Skateboarding: What it is, what skills are required.

7. Story: Anecdote about a skater who once feared the sport.

8. Techniques: How to skate forward, skate backward, turn, speed up, slow down, and stop.

9. Getting started: Things to do first—how to begin if you've never skated in your life.

- Would you drop any of these chunks (subtopics)? If so, which ones?
- Would you reorder anything? If so, how?
- Would you add any new topics? If so, what?

©2009. Allyn & Bacon, a division of Pearson Education. Developed by Vicki Spandel. All rights reserved.

Sample D: Revising with Partners

Good design? Anything out of order?

Public Speaking

1. Disaster! What to do if all goes wrong and you fall, stammer, or trip on the microphone cord.

2. Other phobias: Other things people fear besides public speaking.

3. Keys to Success: The "top 5" things you can do to be successful once you're actually *on stage*.

4. Knowing your topic: The importance of doing your research.

5. Knowing your audience: How to look the audience right in the eye (or eyes).

6. Famous speakers: People who have been successful speakers—what's their secret, anyway??

7. Rehearsal: How to rehearse for the "real thing" (e.g., speak to your plant).

8. Stage Fright: Discussion of how public speaking is one of the biggest fears among the general population.

- Would you drop any of these chunks (subtopics)? If so, which ones?
- Would you reorder anything? If so, how?
- Would you add any new topics? If so, what?

©2009. Allyn & Bacon, a division of Pearson Education. Developed by Vicki Spandel. All rights reserved.

Suggested Revisions of C and D

Sample C: Whole Class Revision

Roller Skating*

1. <u>History</u>: When the sport of roller skating began, how it has changed since the 1700s. *(Formerly #4—A good place to begin because it sets the stage.)*

2. <u>Choosing skates</u>: A guide to choosing roller skates that are comfortable, functional, and durable. *(Formerly #3—A good next topic because you must have skates before you can skate!)*

3. <u>Other equipment</u>: An overview of other equipment you will need, including a helmet and knee pads. *(Formerly #2—A natural follow-up to a discussion of choosing skates.)*

4. <u>Getting started</u>: Things to do first—how to begin if you've never skated in your life. *(Formerly #8—This needs to come early on, to reassure readers new to this sport.)*

5. <u>Falling</u>: Tips for falling properly so you can minimize injury. *(Formerly #1—You don't want this to be the first thing you discuss—but face it, it's a worry. So—time to talk about it.)*

6. <u>Techniques</u>: How to skate forward, skate backward, turn, speed up, slow down, and stop. *(Formerly #7—Now that falling is out of the way, readers will want to know how to do it right.)*

7. <u>Story</u>: Anecdote about a skater who once feared the sport. *(Formerly #7—A good final thought—readers may be nervous, too!)*

---

*We deleted #5 and #6 (skateboarding and ice skating). You *could* find a way to connect these topics, but the report will get VERY long.

©2009. Allyn & Bacon, a division of Pearson Education. Developed by Vicki Spandel. All rights reserved.

Sample D: Revising with Partners

Public Speaking*

1. <u>Stage Fright</u>: Discussion of how public speaking is one
   of the biggest fears among the general population.
   (Formerly #8—This is on everyone's mind, so address it right up front.)

2. <u>Knowing your topic</u>: The importance of doing your
   research. *(Formerly #4—This is the antidote to stage fright, so it fits
   here perfectly.)*

3. <u>Rehearsal</u>: How to rehearse for the "real thing" (e.g.,
   speak to your plant). *(Formerly #7—Once you know your topic,
   you can rehearse, so it fits right here.)*

4. <u>Keys to Success</u>: The "top 5" things you can do to be
   successful once you're actually *on stage*. *(Formerly #3—This
   is the biggest chunk—it needs to go in the middle for balance.)*

5. <u>Knowing your audience</u>: How to look the audience right
   in the eye (or eyes). *(Formerly #5—This topic flows right out of
   "keys to success.")*

6. <u>Disaster</u>! What to do if all goes wrong and you fall,
   stammer, or trip on the microphone cord. *(Formerly #1—
   Raising this issue toward the end leaves anxious, nervous readers with
   a good feeling.)*

7. <u>Famous speakers</u>: People who have been successful
   speakers—what's their secret, anyway?? *(Formerly #6—
   Everyone loves a secret—this makes for a killer ending.)*

---

*Note: "Other Phobias" was deleted. It would just make the report too big.

©2009. Allyn & Bacon, a division of Pearson Education. Developed by Vicki Spandel. All rights reserved.

A Dash of Emphasis

Trait Connection: **Conventions**

Introduction (Share with students in your own words.)

You could live your whole writing life and not use a dash—but it wouldn't be as much fun! See? Dashes let you act. They let you gesture or point. They let you wave your arms and raise your eyebrows and shrug your shoulders—all right there on the page. Dashes show emphasis—or sometimes bewilderment. You can tell when the moment is right for a dash. It's just when you would turn your head and look a listener right in the eye, or raise your hands, palms up, as if to say, "See what I mean?" or "Am I right about this?" The dash draws attention to what follows (or what falls between two dashes), like this:

> She was sick of stewed broccoli—*big* time.
>
> He was certain the dog would never bite him—or *would* it?
>
> Bob had one big goal in life—but he could never recall what it was.
>
> It was raining again—no big surprise—right on his birthday.

Editors call a real dash an *em dash* (it's called that on your computer, too) and they often call for it with a mark that looks like an odd fraction, a *1* over an *m*, like this: $\frac{1}{m}$

We're going to keep things simple and just use a long, lean line: —

An *em dash* is two clicks on the keyboard. This is important because one click is a hyphen, which is another beast altogether. So—let's warm up. Where might you put a dash in each of these three sentences? Put your finger on the spot.

> Amy loved chocolate a *lot* of chocolate.
>
> Sylvester wanted to throw a party but who would come?
>
> The librarian a surly sort of fellow didn't actually like books.

If you read the sentences aloud, slowly, you'll hear yourself pointing a finger at just the right moments. And your sentences will look like this:

Amy loved chocolate—a *lot* of chocolate.

Sylvester wanted to throw a party—but who would come?

The librarian—a surly sort of fellow—didn't actually like books.

Clever editor that you are, you've probably figured out that the dash is optional. Omitting a dash—unlike omitting a comma or period—won't get you into trouble. But—and this is the thing—the dash has dramatic power. With dashes, you can encourage your readers to read your writing with expression and emphasis, just as you wish they would. Periods make them stop. Commas make them pause. But dashes make them hesitate for a moment—and then pounce. *So* much more satisfying for a writer—don't you think?

In the practice that follows, we've left BIG spaces between words so you have room to insert dashes where you like. Don't overdo, but have fun.

Teaching the Lesson (General Guidelines for Teachers)

1. Share the examples above, or make up your own examples to practice inserting dashes for emphasis.

2. Talk about how the dash influences oral reading, and practice reading text with dashes.

3. Share the editing lesson on the following page. Students should read the passage silently and aloud, looking and listening for moments where a dash would create the right emphasis. It helps to point first, before marking up the text.

4. Ask them to edit individually first, then check with a partner. Partners should practice reading aloud (softly) to each other.

5. When everyone is done, ask them to coach you as you edit the same copy.

6. When you finish, read your edited copy aloud, with plenty of dramatic flair, pausing to discuss your choices about where and when to use dashes effectively. Then compare it with our suggested text on page 96.

7. Remember that there are no rights or wrongs to this lesson. However, in some cases, if students choose not to use a dash, they may need a comma (or need to revise) to make the sentence read correctly.

Editing Goal: Use dashes effectively.
Follow-Up: Look for opportunities to use dashes
in your own writing—for emphasis.

Editing Practice

Use dashes (or other punctuation) to create dramatic oral reading.
<u>Hint</u>: We left space for 6. (The final choice is up to you, though.)

Eloise loved to bake pies or tarts or cookies anything at all really. What's more and she often said this herself she was very good at it. People came from miles around to eat her treats. Why not? They were delicious. There was only one small problem and it was not so small, at that. She was running out of money. Baking, after all, costs money lots of money. Then one day, a solution appeared. Mr. Finito, who loved pies above all things on earth, offered to buy Eloise her own pie shop on one condition. She had to bake him a pie of his choice every single day.

©2009. Allyn & Bacon, a division of Pearson Education. Developed by Vicki Spandel. All rights reserved.

Edited Copy

6 dashes added

Eloise loved to bake pies or tarts or cookies— anything at
all really. What's more—and she often said this herself—
she was very good at it. People came from miles around to
eat her treats. Why not? They were delicious. There was
only one small problem—and it was not so small, at that.
She was running out of money. Baking, after all, costs
money—lots of money. Then one day, a solution appeared.
Mr. Finito, who loved pies above all things on earth, offered
to buy Eloise her own pie shop—on one condition. She had
to bake him a pie of his choice every single day.

©2009. Allyn & Bacon, a division of Pearson Education. Developed by Vicki Spandel. All rights reserved.

Revising with a Cliffhanger

Trait Connection: **Organization**

Introduction

Maybe you've found yourself watching a television series when it's the last episode of the season and the hero is in BIG trouble. Maybe he or she is stranded somewhere, or caught in a wild storm—or left to solve some intricate mystery. You want desperately to know how things turn out, but you're told you'll have to wait for the next episode—next season. Such endings are commonly called "cliffhangers," and they can be highly effective. Not only do they keep you tuned in right up until the last moment, but they also encourage you to come back for more. A cliffhanger ending is different from a traditional ending in that it does not tie things up neatly. Quite the opposite, in fact. It leaves things up in the air to set the stage for a new beginning. Cliffhanger endings work especially well at the ends of chapters in a multi-chapter book. They're the endings that make you say, "Read another chapter!" Those clever writers. In this lesson, you'll get to be the clever one who teases the reader.

Teacher's Sidebar . . .

A cliffhanger ending isn't really an ending at all, of course. It's the ultimate transition. Like all good transitions, it forms a connection—sometimes chapter to chapter, sometimes book to book. Cliffhangers are meant to raise questions—and create a little frustration. The main difference between a traditional ending and a cliffhanger ending is that the first answers questions, while the latter raises them. People who cannot keep a secret are seldom good at writing cliffhanger endings.

Focus and Intent

This lesson is intended to help students:

- Understand the concept of a cliffhanger ending.
- Recognize the questions raised by a good cliffhanger.
- Revise a short narrative by replacing a traditional ending with a good cliffhanger ending.

Teaching the Lesson

Step 1: Separating Cliffhangers from Wrap-Ups

Some of the following are cliffhanger endings—and raise more questions than they answer. Others are wrap-up endings, the sort that tie everything up with a bow. Put an X by each cliffhanger ending, and talk about the questions it raises. What do you hope to find out in the next chapter?

____ We spent three nights and four wretched days trying everything we could think of to lash those logs together so they would form a floating raft. Every attempt failed. No sooner did we launch the raft than the logs drifted apart like spaghetti in a boiling pot. As I felt my last bit of hope float away like morning fog, I caught a glimpse of Tad's face. His mouth hadn't broken into a grin yet, but his eyes were smiling—and I knew he'd come up with some crazy idea no one else had thought of.

____ The twenty-mile bicycle race hadn't ended quite the way we thought. None of us had won, or even placed—except for the "long-shot" Glynnis, who had proven herself tougher than many two-legged bikers, and come in a remarkable third. Some people were sorry they had bet against her. I was glad that for once I hadn't.

____ All four of us watched in disbelief as the balloon rose higher and higher, carrying its two passengers off toward the mountain. "Come back!" Mr. Palmer yelled, absurdly, waving his arms and jumping up and down. The very surprised "passengers" didn't know *how* to come back, even if they had wanted to. They didn't even know where they were headed—and unfortunately, neither did we.

____ Who would have thought a one-eyed cat who couldn't catch a mouse or rat to save her life would be the one to rescue us from a fire? Mom didn't say anything, but she reached down and scratched Whisper behind her scruffy ears, and the old cat purred softly. Wherever we were moving to, I knew Whisper would be coming with us.

[Endings 1 and 3 are the cliffhangers, while 2 and 4 offer resolution.]

Step 2: Making the Reading-Writing Connection

Among the most famous of Roald Dahl's many stories is the one commonly referred to as "The Great Mouse Plot," a chapter from his autobiography *Boy*. The story doesn't actually begin with that chapter, however. It begins with the cliffhanger ending of the *preceding* chapter. Dahl has been telling readers about the scrawny, pig-eyed Mrs Pratchett—who has very little time for small boys, despite running a candy shop that lures them in. Oh, how they would *love* to have some revenge for the wretched treatment they've suffered at her filthy hands—and here's the ending that sets it up:

So you can well understand that we had it in for Mrs Pratchett in a big way, but we didn't quite know what to do about it. Many schemes were put forward, but none of them was any good. None of them, that is, until suddenly, one memorable afternoon, we found the dead mouse.

(From *Boy* by Roald Dahl. 1999. New York: Puffin. Page 34.)

Would *you* want to stop at this point? Most readers don't. Dahl knows all too well that we want to know what the boys do with that dead mouse—and he uses our curiosity to propel us right into the next chapter. If Dahl had been *ending* his story of Mrs Pratchett right then and there, he might have written this last line: *We never did come up with a way of getting back at her—but perhaps it's just as well because we all stayed out of trouble.* But who would read the next chapter after a deadly dull line like that?

Step 3: Involving Students as Evaluators

Ask students to review Samples A and B, specifically considering which writer has created a cliffhanger ending, and which has gone for a more traditional ending. Have students work with a partner, noting the questions that the cliffhanger ending raises and thinking of a cliffhanger alternative for the traditional ending.

Discussing Results

Most students should identify Sample B as the one with the cliffhanger ending. Sample A wraps things up neatly—but B does not. A possible cliffhanger ending for Sample A is provided.

Step 4: Modeling Revision

- Share Sample C (*Whole Class Revision*) with students. Read it aloud.
- Talk about whether the writer of Sample C has used a traditional or cliffhanger ending. (Most students should say *traditional*.) Invite students to coach you through a class revision of the ending, first talking through how much to cut (cross out)—and then writing a new cliffhanger ending to replace what you delete. (Hint: Think about where you'd like the next chapter to pick up.)
- When you finish, read through the entire story, new ending and all. Do you like the questions your new ending raises? Can you imagine where and how you would begin to write the next chapter? If you wish, compare your cliffhanger ending with ours, remembering that yours need not match ours in any way.

Step 5: Revising with Partners

Pass out copies of Sample D (*Revising with Partners*). Ask students to follow the basic steps you modeled with Sample C. *Working with partners*, they should:

- Read the piece aloud.

- Talk about whether the writer has used a traditional or a cliffhanger ending.

- Talk through ways of revising the ending to make it a cliffhanger—thinking especially about questions they'd like to raise in the reader's mind.

- Create a cliffhanger ending by crossing out as much of the original as they would like and rewriting, inventing any needed details.

- Read the result aloud to hear the difference.

Step 6: Sharing and Discussing Results

When students have finished, ask several pairs of students to share their cliffhanger endings aloud. How many different endings did your students, as a class, come up with? Which ending leaves readers most eager for the next installment? (Feel free to share our suggested revision, keeping in mind that students' revisions need not match ours in any way.)

Next Steps

- You can turn *any* ending into a cliffhanger by leaving things up in the air. Practice on endings from chapters or books, using any favorite literature.

- When students share narratives in response groups, ask writers to read everything *up to the ending*—then *stop*. Invite listeners to write a cliffhanger ending on a 3×5 card and turn all cards in to the writer—who is free to use any (or none) of the ideas in crafting a final ending.

- Listen and look for cliffhanger endings in the literature you share aloud. Notice chapter endings in particular—because these cliffhangers guide you into the next chapter. Recommended:
  - *Boy* by Roald Dahl. 1999. New York: Puffin.
  - *A Dog's Life* by Ann M. Martin. 2005. New York: Scholastic.
  - *Holes* by Louis Sachar. 1998. New York: Random House.
  - *Peter and the Starcatchers* by Dave Barry and Ridley Pearson. 2006. New York: Hyperion Paperbacks for Children.

- *For an additional challenge:* Once students have written cliffhanger endings for several stories in this lesson, invite students who are ready to take the next step to write the follow-up installment for any story.

Sample A

New Teacher

What had he gotten into? Sam had just been thinking how cool it would be to make a few bucks, and when the "tutor" position came up, he pictured himself explaining math to some small kid in a corner—or maybe coaching a student through a geography lesson. Now here he was, with six adults staring at him, waiting for him to explain English to them. He had no idea what to do, and his heart was racing about a thousand beats a minute. They waited and smiled. He smiled back. Finally, slowly, he put one hand on his chest. "I'm Sam," he said. They became very quiet, and he realized they were straining to hear him. "Sam," he said louder, slapping his chest vigorously.

"Sam!" they all yelled back, slapping their chests. Sam couldn't help himself. He burst out laughing, and so did the group.

Slowly, Sam got them to understand that he was asking for their names. They went around the group, one by one, patting themselves as they spoke . . . *Rosa . . . Marquesa . . . Dierdre . . . Chin Lee . . . Akira . . . Dafne.* Sam made name tags, printing their names in big letters. They went round again—then practiced saying each other's names—and his. Before the night was done, they had named almost every object in the room, and Sam had put labels on everything, using the whole pack of 3×5 cards he had somehow thought to bring with him. Suddenly, it hit him that it was ten past eight—they had run ten minutes over schedule, and he hadn't even noticed. He shook everyone's hand as they filed out the door, unable to believe how well things had gone. This nightmare had turned into his dream job. He loved it!

©2009. Allyn & Bacon, a division of Pearson Education. Developed by Vicki Spandel. All rights reserved.

Sample B

Fire Fighter

Chelsea was seriously out of breath. The volunteers were scrambling to make it out across the ridge before the fire could meet them coming up the other way, and she wasn't sure she would make it. The hill was steep. A giant pillow of pine needles, accumulated over dozens of years, gave way constantly beneath her feet, causing her to slide back. Thick underbrush clawed at her heavy, protective clothing. It was only that clothing that disguised her identity. She was the only girl on the crew, and at 14, she was by far the youngest person out here—much too young to be admitted as a volunteer. When the emergency call had come into the fire station from the lookout tower, everyone was too busy rushing around to notice who was who—and slipping into someone else's uniform had been easy—and had seemed wildly exciting at the time.

Breathing heavily, Chelsea whirled around, grabbing a small pine tree to balance herself, and looking for the others. The roar of the fire was deafening, and she realized with a jolt that her climbing efforts had taken her over 400 yards from the rest of the crew. One of them had spotted her and was waving frantically and pointing. She could not make out what he was saying—until she looked up. The fire had crested, right above her. Flames were leaping tree to tree. Gasping for air, Chelsea half ran, half stumbled toward the crew, hearing the roar build behind her. Her knees were buckling, her feet felt heavy as stones. *Don't fall*, she told herself. *Whatever you do, don't fall*. There was a crash—then darkness.

©2009. Allyn & Bacon, a division of Pearson Education. Developed by Vicki Spandel. All rights reserved.

Cliffhanger? or Traditional?

Suggested Revision of Sample A

What had he gotten into? Sam had just been thinking how cool it would be to make a few bucks, and when the "tutor" position came up, he pictured himself explaining math to some small kid in a corner—or maybe coaching a student through a geography lesson. Now here he was, with six adults staring at him, waiting for him to explain English to them. He had no idea what to do, and his heart was racing about a thousand beats a minute. They waited and smiled. He smiled back. Finally, slowly, he put one hand on his chest. "I'm Sam," he said. They became very quiet, and he realized they were straining to hear him. "Sam," he said louder, slapping his chest vigorously.

"Sam!" they all yelled back, slapping their chests. Sam couldn't help himself. He burst out laughing, and so did the group.

Slowly, Sam got them to understand that he was asking for their names. They went around the group, one by one, patting themselves as they spoke . . . *Rosa . . . Marquesa . . . Dierdre . . . Chin Lee . . . Akira . . . Dafne*. Sam made name tags, printing their names in big letters. They went round again—then practiced saying each other's names—and his. Before the night was done, they had named almost every object in the room, and Sam had put labels on everything, using the whole pack of 3×5 cards he had somehow thought to bring with him. Suddenly, it hit him that it was ten past eight—they had run ten minutes over schedule, and he hadn't even noticed. He shook everyone's hand as they filed out the door, ~~unable to believe how well things had gone. This nightmare had turned into his dream job. He loved it,~~ thinking to himself that his little pack of labeling cards had saved him for one night—but what on earth would he do tomorrow? One thing he knew for sure—he had to come up with a dynamite idea because he could not afford to lose this job.

©2009. Allyn & Bacon, a division of Pearson Education. Developed by Vicki Spandel. All rights reserved.

Sample C: Whole Class Revision

Nuts and Bolts

If he hadn't been so pig-headed about going to the concert, and *if* he hadn't taken the car—when his dad had specifically asked him not to—Nick wouldn't be in this fix. Or so he thought to himself, as he sat on a rock, beside a deserted road, looking at his flat tire. *If.* Well, too late for if. Too late for wishing or hindsight. Time to do something. He'd seen his dad change tires plenty of times, though he had never done it himself.

He popped the trunk and found a wrench for loosening the lug nuts that held the wheels on the car. He also found the jack—and figured out how to work it. Remembering something else he'd seen his dad do, Nick scouted out some big rocks and used them to brace the other tires so the car wouldn't roll. He made sure the parking brake was on, and slipped the ignition key into his pocket. He tugged the spare out of the trunk, laid it on the ground, and sighed. "Here goes nothing, he mumbled," starting to loosen one of the lug nuts. It wouldn't budge. He twisted harder. Then harder still.

Moving to the side of the car, Nick carefully placed the jack under the metal plate and started pumping. He almost laughed aloud when the car eased up. It was simpler than he'd thought. In no time, he had the old tire off and the new one on. He put the tools away, closed up the trunk, and headed for home. Whew! He was so relieved to have everything turn out OK.

©2009. Allyn & Bacon, a division of Pearson Education. Developed by Vicki Spandel. All rights reserved.

Sample D: Revising with Partners

Explorers

Of all the games they played together over the summer, Rumor and Hannah liked "explorer" best. The rules were simple: (1) You had to go somewhere you hadn't been before, (2) If the other person dared you to do something, you had to do it no matter how disgusting or scary it might be, and (3) Once you accepted a dare, there was no turning back until the expedition was finished. They had swum to an island, waded through a mucky swamp, and slept overnight in the middle of a cow pasture.

Now they stood at the edge of an old dump, filled with tires, trash, and who knew what else. It was fenced with eight-foot chain link, and the gate was locked. They looked at each other, and Hannah wiped soot from her face, biting her lip. They knew what the other was thinking—they always knew. As soon as one of them dared the other to go in, there was no turning back. Right now, they could still turn around and head home—which would be the smart thing to do. The safe thing. Just then, something moved inside one of the tires. Rumor saw it first, and squinted, trying to make it out. It moved again—and before she could stop herself, the words were out of her mouth.

"Let's just go home," she said to Hannah, grabbing her friend's arm. Hannah nodded, and they turned around and headed back together. After all, there would be other days to do dares, and it felt good to be safe.

©2009. Allyn & Bacon, a division of Pearson Education. Developed by Vicki Spandel. All rights reserved.

Suggested Revisions of C and D

Sample C: Whole Class Revision

Nuts and Bolts

If he hadn't been so pig-headed about going to the concert, and *if* he hadn't taken the car—when his dad had specifically asked him not to—Nick wouldn't be in this fix. Or so he thought to himself, as he sat on a rock, beside a deserted road, looking at his flat tire. *If.* Well, too late for if. Too late for wishing or hindsight. Time to do something. He'd seen his dad change tires plenty of times, though he had never done it himself.

He popped the trunk and found a wrench for loosening the lug nuts that held the wheels on the car. He also found the jack—and figured out how to work it. Remembering something else he'd seen his dad do, Nick scouted out some big rocks and used them to brace the other tires so the car wouldn't roll. He made sure the parking brake was on, and slipped the ignition key into his pocket. He tugged the spare out of the trunk, laid it on the ground, and sighed. "Here goes nothing, he mumbled," starting to loosen one of the lug nuts. It wouldn't budge. He twisted harder. Then harder still.

Moving to the side of the car, Nick carefully placed the jack under the metal plate and started pumping. He almost laughed aloud when the car eased up. It was simpler than he'd thought. ~~In no time, he had the old tire off and the new one on. He put the tools away, closed up the trunk and headed for home. Whew! He was so relieved to have everything turn out OK.~~ What he could not seem to do was loosen the old tire. He'd thought he felt it give, but now it seemed tighter than ever. He jumped on the cross wrench—but it wouldn't budge! It was getting dark. Nick's cell phone was out of range. He lowered the car, climbed back in, locked the doors, and turned on the radio. No reception. There <u>had</u> to be a way out of this. He had always been a good problem solver. He would think of <u>something</u>.

©2009. Allyn & Bacon, a division of Pearson Education. Developed by Vicki Spandel. All rights reserved.

Sample D: Revising with Partners

Explorers

Of all the games they played together over the summer, Rumor and Hannah liked "explorer" best. The rules were simple: (1) You had to go somewhere you hadn't been before, (2) If the other person dared you to do something, you had to do it no matter how disgusting or scary it might be, and (3) Once you accepted a dare, there was no turning back until the expedition was finished. They had swum to an island, waded through a mucky swamp, and slept overnight in the middle of a cow pasture.

Now they stood at the edge of an old dump, filled with tires, trash, and who knew what else. It was fenced with eight-foot chain link, and the gate was locked. They looked at each other, and Hannah wiped soot from her face, biting her lip. They knew what the other was thinking— they always knew. As soon as one of them dared the other to go in, there was no turning back. Right now, they could still turn around and head home—which would be the smart thing to do. The safe thing. Just then, something moved inside one of the tires. Rumor saw it first, and squinted, trying to make it out. It moved again—and before she could stop herself, the words were out of her mouth.

~~"Let's just go home," she said to Hannah, grabbing her friend's arm. Hannah nodded, and they turned around and headed back together. After all, there would be other days to do dares, and it felt good to be safe.~~

"I double dog dare you to go over that fence," she whispered to Hannah, who stared back. Hannah hesitated for a full minute, then took a jump at the fence and began to climb. Rumor watched her friend inch up. Hannah was an expert climber, and unafraid of heights. In the corner of her eye, Rumor could see that movement again, and she called out to her friend, who was now near the top—"Hannah, wait!" But it was too late.

©2009. Allyn & Bacon, a division of Pearson Education. Developed by Vicki Spandel. All rights reserved.

Nonessential (but interesting)

Trait Connection: **Conventions**

Introduction (Share with students in your own words.)

The dash—as we've seen so well—is a bold, extroverted mark of punctuation that lives to point things out:

> She could drive—but she couldn't steer.
>
> Bob was out of money—but not out of ideas.
>
> Ted—who had actually taken the money—accused Sylvia of theft.

While the dash is busy pointing fingers, parentheses are quietly whispering in the reader's ear. "Excuse me," they say, "this isn't *vital*, but I'll tell you just in case you're interested." Information that comes wrapped in parentheses is not essential to the sentence. It could be omitted—but like a secret whispered in your ear, it might be of interest:

> Fred (a former teacher) had moved to Alaska to photograph wildlife.
>
> Ed's Market (which had opened in 1917) did more business than almost any other grocery store in town.
>
> Hamburgers, sandwiches, and salads (along with other items) have been dropped from our menu.

When deciding between a dash and parentheses (which always come in pairs, by the way), ask yourself, "Is this something I'm trying to point out, as if I were a tour guide pointing to a famous painting? Or, is this something I'm whispering as an aside because, though interesting, it's not critical." That key question will tell you what to do.

As you saw in the last lesson, dashes are optional—though they have flair and panache, and you wouldn't want to do without them forever. Parentheses are usually optional, too, especially when you're whispering a comment in the reader's ear. Sometimes, though, you really need them, when referencing a chapter or other resource, or when numbering items in a series:

1. The elephant is highly intelligent and capable of emotion (see Chapter 4).

2. Orangutans are (1) brighter than most other primates, (2) extremely shy for animals that are so strong, and (3) tender, loving parents.

In the practice that follows, we'll focus on the first use of parentheses—for nonessential information that adds a tidbit to a sentence.

Teaching the Lesson (General Guidelines for Teachers)

1. Share the examples above, or make up your own examples to practice inserting parentheses when setting off a nonessential comment.

2. Talk about how the parentheses influence oral reading, and practice reading text with parentheses aloud.

3. Share the editing lesson on the following page. Students should read the passage silently and aloud, looking and listening for moments where parentheses would effectively enclose nonessential information.

4. Ask them to edit individually first, then check with a partner. Partners should practice reading aloud (softly) to each other.

5. When everyone is done, ask them to coach you as you edit the same copy.

6. When you finish, read your edited copy aloud, lowering your voice to show how parentheses set off information not vital to the core sentence. Compare your edited copy with our suggested text on page 111.

7. Remember that there are no rights or wrongs to this lesson. However, if students choose not to use parentheses, they may need commas to make their sentences read correctly.

**Editing Goal: Use parentheses effectively. (We left
room for 8 pairs of parentheses in this lesson.)
Follow-Up: Look for opportunities to use parentheses
in your own writing (for nonessentials).**

Editing Practice

Use parentheses (or other punctuation) to set off nonessential information.
<u>Hint</u>: We left space for 8 pairs of parentheses.

Brett loved the film "Pirates of the Caribbean" the first

edition and had seen it at least ten times possibly twelve .

His sister Jennifer—who detested pirates—had never seen

it no big disappointment . Jennifer a 4.0 student spent a

lot of time reading—mostly nonfiction nothing about

pirates . She also played the piano jazz mostly . Brett was

proud of his sister, but wasn't about to give up pirates for

her or for anybody . He didn't picture himself taking up

the piano, either . They seemed headed down different

equally interesting paths .

©2009. Allyn & Bacon, a division of Pearson Education. Developed by Vicki Spandel. All rights reserved.

Edited Copy

8 pairs of parentheses added
Parenthetical phrases are underlined so they stand out.

Brett loved the film "Pirates of the Caribbean" (the first edition) and had seen it at least ten times (possibly twelve). His sister Jennifer—who detested pirates—had never seen it (no big disappointment). Jennifer (a 4.0 student) spent a lot of time reading—mostly nonfiction (nothing about pirates). She also played the piano (jazz mostly). Brett was proud of his sister, but wasn't about to give up pirates for her (or for anybody). He didn't picture himself taking up the piano, either. They seemed headed down different (equally interesting) paths.

> **Note**
> Most writers would never use parentheses this often. We have done so for purposes of practice and illustration.

©2009. Allyn & Bacon, a division of Pearson Education. Developed by Vicki Spandel. All rights reserved.

Revising from Within

Trait Connection: **Voice**

Introduction

We are thinking, all of us, nonstop. Of course, not everything we think goes public—in either spoken *or* written form. That's probably a very good thing. Still, voice comes, ultimately, from those innermost thoughts. Voice is who we are. It's the presence of the writer on the page. Good writers learn to free some of those innermost thoughts in order to let readers in on their thinking. To show what's going on inside a *character's* mind, a writer will sometimes use italics, *slanted print*. This sets those inside thoughts apart from what characters say or do—which is then shown in Roman (straight-up) print. As we'll see in this lesson, getting in on someone's thinking, or *internal monologue*, boosts voice—especially when the person says precisely what is on his or her mind, no holding back.

Teacher's Sidebar . . .

The technique of sharing inner thoughts—sometimes called *internal monologue*—is most effective in situations where the character is stressed, or does not feel free to say what he or she thinks aloud. Roald Dahl's book *The BFG*, for example, begins in a dormitory, where Sophie is unable to sleep. She gets up to peer out the window at the moonlit night—and sees something that takes her breath away. Roald Dahl could simply have told us what Sophie was thinking—using words like "Sophie thought to herself . . ." But that would not have had the chilling immediacy of internal monologue, which lets us think right along *with* Sophie, as she slowly realizes what she sees:

Suddenly, she froze. *There was something coming up the street on the opposite side. It was something black . . .*
Something tall and black . . .
Something very tall and very black and very thin . . .

(Roald Dahl. *The BFG*. 2007. New York: Puffin. Page 11. Italics in original.)

Focus and Intent

This lesson is intended to help students:

- Appreciate the power of sharing a character's thoughts.
- Practice sharing thoughts in italic form.
- Revise a short piece to include stronger internal monologue.

Teaching the Lesson

Step 1: Creating Italic Thoughts

Following are several brief scenarios in which a character is likely having thoughts he or she is reluctant to share out loud. Imagine what each character might be thinking, and write it out, using *italics* or underlining. Be inventive; let your characters speak freely. The first example is done for you.

1. Jake was dumbfounded when the teacher accused him of cheating. He had put Denise's list of answers into his backpack to *protect* her—and she now sat staring at her test paper as if nothing had happened. Mr. Chillworth had taken Jake's test paper, and was now shredding it into paper flakes over the wastebasket. Jake kept staring at Denise's bowed head.

    [Jake's thoughts]

    Speak up! Why don't you speak up?

2. Melissa had wanted so much to be on the basketball team—but she had spent most of this game sitting on the bench. Cheering wasn't enough. She wanted in. Her team was behind by six points, and the other team was coming on hard. It was almost the end of the third quarter . . .

    [Melissa's thoughts]

    _____

3. He probably should have called a long time ago. But apologizing was always *so* hard. Ray couldn't even recall exactly what he'd said before Phil turned and took off running. He hadn't seen him since that day, but now he just hoped Phil would listen to what he had to say. The phone rang once, twice . . .

    [Ray's thoughts]

    _____

Step 2: Making the Reading-Writing Connection

In *Jack's Black Book*, narrator Jack Henry longs to be a writer. He decides to begin by writing a novel, but the muses just won't visit him—though he is certain they come to every other writer who stares at the ceiling, searching for ideas:

> But the more I stared at the cracks in my ceiling while dressed in a terry-cloth bathrobe, sucking on my lead pencil point with my ears perked up like a Chihuahua's, the only ideas that rolled around in my empty head were ugly. *Give up. Throw in the towel. You don't have what it takes to write a novel.* My stupidity was stalking me like some big dumb monster with a club.

> (From *Jack's Black Book* by Jack Gantos. 1999. New York: Farrar, Straus, and Giroux. Page 5.)

Read the internal monologue—the part in italics—aloud again. Have you ever had thoughts like these? *Most* writers have. This is why we laugh when Jack shares so openly what's going on in his head. Notice how uncompromising Jack's thoughts are—he doesn't soften them in any way. What if the "big, dumb monster" in Jack's head had said, "Well, maybe I'm not cut out to be a writer. No big deal"? Would that have had as much impact?

Step 3: Involving Students as Evaluators

Ask students to review Samples A and B, looking for the internal monologue in italics, and specifically considering which writer has more effectively used internal monologue to create voice. Have students work with a partner, noting precisely where we get inside each character's head and asking whether they might have written something different to express the character's thoughts.

Discussing Results

Most students should identify Sample B as stronger. While the writer of Sample A uses internal dialogue, it is not particularly strong or honest. A possible revision of Sample A is provided.

Step 4: Modeling Revision

- Share Sample C (*Whole Class Revision*) with students. Read it aloud, identifying the internal monologue.

- Talk about whether the writer of Sample C has used internal monologue effectively. (Most students should say *no.*) Invite students to coach you through a class revision, first talking through what this person is *really* thinking—and how that could be honestly and directly expressed. Write out your thoughts in italics—remembering that in handwritten copy, italics can be indicated simply by underlining.

- When you finish, read through the entire piece, italicized thoughts and all. Did you allow your character to speak with enough force and honesty to give the piece voice? If you wish, compare your revision with ours, remembering that yours need not match ours in any way.

Step 5: Revising with Partners

Pass out copies of Sample D (*Revising with Partners*). Ask students to follow the basic steps you modeled with Sample C. *Working with partners,* they should:

- Read the piece aloud and identify lines of internal monologue.
- Talk about whether that monologue is effective—or a bit weak.
- Talk through ways of revising that monologue to make it stronger—asking what is *really* going on in the character's head.
- Create new internal monologue with stronger voice.
- Read the result aloud to hear the difference.

Step 6: Sharing and Discussing Results

When students have finished, ask several pairs of students to share their revisions aloud. Are teams' internal monologues very different? Which are the most forceful? Which create the strongest voice? (Feel free to share our suggested revision, keeping in mind that students' revisions need not match ours in any way.)

Next Steps

- Sometimes we think we know what a character is thinking because of what he or she says or does. Test your intuition. Literature offers numerous opportunities to create internal monologue even when it is not provided by the author. Ask students to choose a favorite scene from any favorite book, and to write a few lines of internal monologue for one or more of the characters.

- When students share narratives in response groups, ask them to pause at a crucial point for one of the characters, without sharing what that character is thinking. Invite each listener to create a single line of internal monologue for that character on a 3×5 card, and turn it in to the writer—who may then use any or none of those internal monologues in the final draft.

- Listen and look for internal monologue in the literature you share aloud. Notice how in almost every case, the writer achieves a slightly different purpose with this monologue. Recommended:
  - *The BFG* by Roald Dahl. 2007. New York: Puffin. (Notice what happens in Sophie's head, and how it influences how we respond to events.)
  - *Jack's Black Book* by Jack Gantos. 1999. New York: Farrar, Straus, and Giroux. (Notice how Jack often goes to great lengths *not* to share his innermost thoughts—except with readers, of course!)
  - *Peter and the Starcatchers* by Dave Barry and Ridley Pearson. 2006. New York: Hyperion Paperbacks for Children. (Listen to the ongoing moments of internal monologue by Captain Scott and Black Stache, pages 114-115.)
  - *Rules* by Cynthia Lord. 2006. New York: Scholastic. (Listen to the phone call, page 183.)
  - *Sing a Song of Tuna Fish* by Esmé Raji Codell. 2004. New York: Hyperion Paperbacks for Children. (Listen to Esmé's painfully conflicted feelings about whether her parents should divorce, page 111.)

- *For an additional challenge:* Once students have had practice writing internal monologue for another character, invite them to try it in a personal narrative, in which they tell a story in their *own* voice. This is more challenging—because it is more personal. But the reward, in terms of the voice achieved, is great.

Sample A

Strong
Monologue?

Off Limits

Of all the places in the school that were off limits, none was more off limits than the counselor's office with its imposing steel cliff of file cabinets. Cabinets that housed the records of all the students in the school—grades, behavioral charts, test scores, and comments, all were behind lock and key in those drawers. Usually. But on this day, the counselor had stepped out just for a few minutes—leaving his door open and the file cabinets unlocked.

Brian knew if he were caught, the consequences would be extremely unpleasant. He'd almost certainly be suspended, perhaps kicked off the football team. On the other hand, if no one came in, he could get the information he was looking for.

He shuffled quickly through the files and found his name. His fingers were trembling so much he could barely separate the papers. He thought he heard a noise in the hallway. *I hope no one comes in right now.*

©2009. Allyn & Bacon, a division of Pearson Education. Developed by Vicki Spandel. All rights reserved.

Sample B

Strong
Monologue?

Jealousy

This is stupid. Stupid, stupid, stupid. Andrea couldn't seem to shut off the feelings, though. It made her crazy when Dix (whose real name was Dixon) would talk to other girls. *Stop it. Think about something else. Yeah, right. Like what?*

He wasn't even in most of her classes. Only math. But she would see him in the hallway or out on the school grounds. Dix was definitely not the best looking boy in the school. That honor went to Carter. But Dix had an irresistible smile. He was amazing at football and even better at math.

He was disorganized, that was for sure. It was one of the best things about him, though, since he always had to borrow a pencil, and that was the only time he and Andrea spoke. "Hey, Andrea, could I borrow a pencil?" he'd ask. Every math class, he asked the same thing. He never, even once, brought a pencil of his own.

"Sure, Dix," Andrea would answer, handing him the pencil she'd had already sharpened for him. *What do you do with your pencils, eat them?*

"Thanks!" he'd say with a grin. And as Andrea smiled back, he would turn and talk to Hannah, the smartest girl in math class. *Hey—Mr. I-never-have-my-own-pencil!! Would it absolutely kill you to talk to me for just one minute?*

©2009. Allyn & Bacon, a division of Pearson Education. Developed by Vicki Spandel. All rights reserved.

Suggested Revision of Sample A

Off Limits

Of all the places in the school that were off limits, none was more off limits than the counselor's office with its imposing steel cliff of file cabinets. Cabinets that housed the records of all the students in the school—grades, behavioral charts, test scores, and comments, all were behind lock and key in those drawers. Usually. But on this day, the counselor had stepped out just for a few minutes—leaving his door open and the file cabinets unlocked.

Brian knew if he were caught, the consequences would be extremely unpleasant. He'd almost certainly be suspended, perhaps kicked off the football team. On the other hand, if no one came in, he could get the information he was looking for. *This will only take a minute . . . it could be the only chance I'll get.*

I can't believe I'm doing this . . . I must be crazy . . .

He shuffled quickly through the files and found his name. His fingers were trembling so much he could barely separate the papers. He thought he heard a noise in the hallway. ~~I hope no one comes in right now.~~ *Whoever you are, don't come in . . . How am I going to explain this???*

©2009. Allyn & Bacon, a division of Pearson Education. Developed by Vicki Spandel. All rights reserved.

Sample C: Whole Class Revision

Friends

Trish and Lisa had been best friends since kindergarten. They had taken swimming lessons together, learned to ride bikes together. They slept over at each other's houses. They liked—and disliked—all the same foods. So when Trish invited Lisa to camp out in her back yard, it wasn't any big surprise. As Trish explained to Sara, "The tent I got for my birthday just isn't big enough for three."

Sara smiled and nodded. "Sure," she said, "I understand."

"I'll ask you another time," Trish added, laughing and tugging on Lisa's arm.

"That would be great," Sara answered, turning so they wouldn't see the tears forming in her eyes. *I hope I don't cry.*

"Have a great time!" she called over her shoulder, walking fast as if she had somewhere important to go.

©2009. Allyn & Bacon, a division of Pearson Education. Developed by Vicki Spandel. All rights reserved.

Sample D: Revising with Partners

Strong
Monologue?

Narrow Escape

When Frankie set out to deliver a package on his bike, he did *not*
anticipate being attacked by a miserable, rat-tailed, half-wild dog. The
dog, a smallish black knot of muscle with eyes so close together he
looked almost like a Cyclops, ran feverishly at Frankie's front tire,
grabbing it viciously in his yellow teeth, and causing the bike to wobble
precipitously.

"Nice dog, nice dog," Frankie said softly, hoping to quiet this
monster with unwashed fur. *I sure hope he goes away!*

The dog was running alongside the bike now, snapping at
Frankie's feet, and growling ominously. Saliva flew from his mouth. He
had no collar. His eyes were burning coals, and across his shoulders,
Frankie could see scars from many fights. "Easy, boy," Frankie crooned,
pushing at the pedals with everything in him.

He could see the top of the hill now, and was pretty sure if he
made it to the other side, he could go fast enough downhill to lose this
unwanted companion. He stood up on the pedals and gave it all he had,
and the dog leaped for his leg.

©2009. Allyn & Bacon, a division of Pearson Education. Developed by Vicki Spandel. All rights reserved.

Suggested Revisions of C and D

Sample C: Whole Class Revision

Friends

Trish and Lisa had been best friends since kindergarten. They had taken swimming lessons together, learned to ride bikes together. They slept over at each other's houses. They liked—and disliked—all the same foods. So when Trish invited Lisa to camp out in her back yard, it wasn't any big surprise. As Trish explained to Sara, "The tent I got for my birthday just isn't big enough for three."

Sara smiled and nodded. "Sure," she said, "I understand."

Actually I don't understand at all.

"I'll ask you another time," Trish added, laughing and tugging on Lisa's arm. ***Sure you will.***

"That would be great," Sara answered, turning so they wouldn't

I have to get out of here before they see me cry.

see the tears forming in her eyes. ~~I hope I don't cry~~

"Have a great time!" she called over her shoulder, walking fast as if she had somewhere important to go. ***Who needs a tent full of mice and ants anyway?***

©2009. Allyn & Bacon, a division of Pearson Education. Developed by Vicki Spandel. All rights reserved.

Sample D: Revising with Partners

Narrow Escape

When Frankie set out to deliver a package on his bike, he did *not*

anticipate being attacked by a miserable, rat-tailed, half-wild dog. The

dog, a smallish black knot of muscle with eyes so close together he

looked almost like a Cyclops, ran feverishly at Frankie's front tire,

grabbing it viciously in his yellow teeth, and causing the bike to wobble

precipitously.

"Nice dog, nice dog," Frankie said softly, hoping to quiet this

Go chomp on someone else's foot!

monster with unwashed fur. ~~I sure hope he goes away!~~

The dog was running alongside the bike now, snapping at

Frankie's feet, and growling ominously. Saliva flew from his mouth. He

had no collar. His eyes were burning coals, and across his shoulders,

Frankie could see scars from many fights. "Easy, boy," Frankie crooned,

pushing at the pedals with everything in him. *Go chase a rattlesnake,*

would ya? A big one . . .

He could see the top of the hill now, and was pretty sure if he made

it to the other side, he could go fast enough downhill to lose this unwanted

companion. He stood up on the pedals and gave it all he had, and the dog

leaped for his leg. *Too bad, pest! Dinner's about to ride away!*

©2009. Allyn & Bacon, a division of Pearson Education. Developed by Vicki Spandel. All rights reserved.

Now for a Brief Pause . . .

Trait Connection: **Conventions**

Introduction (Share with students in your own words.)

Get ready. Here comes another mark, called the ellipsis, that is often (like the dash and the parentheses) *optional*. Notice we said often—but not always. Let's get the exception out of the way first.

The ellipsis, which consists of three dots (. . .), is used in a quotation to show that words have been deliberately left out. Let's say you wish to quote from a book jacket for your favorite novel, but you don't want to use the entire first sentence. You just want to make a quick point. Your quotation might look like this:

"This novel is . . . destined to be a classic."

Obviously, the writer whom you're quoting said a bit more—but you got what you wanted, and by using the ellipsis, you also let the reader know some words were missing. That's the courteous thing to do—as well as the accurate thing.

An ellipsis has another, very interesting use, however—and this one is optional. Still, once you learn it, you'll wonder how you did without it. That's because it allows writing to imitate speech. Sometimes, when you're speaking, do you find yourself searching for the right word or phrase? You might pause . . . and you could use ellipsis to show that pause, just like this:

Wilbur wasn't the worst cat in the world . . . but he came *close*.

I . . . I never *meant* to shoot her.

Obviously, only the writer can know when he or she means to create dramatic pauses such as these. The repetition of the pronoun "I" really does call for an ellipsis, though some writers might use a dash. In the first example about Wilbur the cat, however, a comma or dash could substitute for the ellipsis. How then, you may ask (in your most editorial voice) am I ever supposed to know which mark to use? Simple. Read the piece aloud, asking yourself, "How do I want the reader to read this?" You have to think whether you want a small pause (comma), or a really big dramatic pause almost like a sigh (ellipsis), or you want to point a finger at something vital (dash) or whisper something not so vital (parentheses).

In the practice that follows, we'll offer you a chance to use the ellipsis three times—and only to show drama, slow motion, or a long deep-breath sort of pause. You don't need to add *any other* punctuation (that challenge comes next time). But you do need to think about where those long pauses fit best. Insert an ellipsis by using a widened caret and tucking the three dots right inside, like this:

The tall figure came closer and closer and closer.

Teaching the Lesson (General Guidelines for Teachers)

1. Share the examples above, or make up your own examples to practice inserting an ellipsis to show a dramatic pause or hesitation.

2. Talk about how an ellipsis influences oral reading, and practice reading text with ellipses aloud. Remind students that this particular mark of punctuation is not used very often.

3. Share the editing lesson on the following page. Students should read the passage silently and aloud, looking and listening for moments where a dramatic pause would be appropriate, and inserting an ellipsis in those spots to influence the reader's interpretation of the passage.

4. Ask them to edit individually first, then check with a partner. Partners should practice reading aloud (softly) to each other.

5. When everyone is done, ask them to coach you as you edit the same copy.

6. When you finish, read your edited copy aloud, pausing very dramatically to show how an ellipsis creates a break in thought or speech. Compare your edited copy with our suggested text on page 126.

7. Remember that there are no rights or wrongs to this lesson. However, the use (or non-use) of ellipsis affects oral reading.

**Editing Goal: Use the ellipsis effectively. Three opportunities are provided.
Follow-Up: Look for opportunities to use ellipses in your own writing
(to create a dramatic pause).**

Editing Practice

Use an ellipsis to indicate a dramatic pause.
<u>Hint</u>: **We created opportunities for 3 ellipses.**

I did not know what to make of Claudia's behavior. She had seemed so so *strange* lately. Each day at 4 sharp, she left the house. I decided to follow her, and see if I could figure out what was going on. She was fast. I had to run to keep up. Then suddenly, Claudia shot around a corner—and simply vanished. Just like that. Poof! "Claudia!" I cried. No response. Glumly, I sat down on the curb and waited and waited. After what felt like an hour, I heard the man at the fish market yelling something about a "four-legged thief." I jumped to my feet. That's when I saw Claudia dodging traffic, carrying *something* or other in her mouth why, a *fish*, of all things!

©2009. Allyn & Bacon, a division of Pearson Education. Developed by Vicki Spandel. All rights reserved.

Edited Copy

3 ellipses added

I did not know what to make of Claudia's behavior. She had

seemed so so *strange* lately. Each day at 4 sharp, she left

the house. I decided to follow her, and see if I could figure

out what was going on. She was fast. I had to run to keep

up. Then suddenly, Claudia shot around a corner—and

simply vanished. Just like that. Poof! "Claudia!" I cried. No

response. Glumly, I sat down on the curb and waited and

waited. After what felt like an hour, I heard the man at the

fish market yelling something about a "four-legged thief."

I jumped to my feet. That's when I saw Claudia dodging

traffic, carrying *something* or other in her mouth why, a

fish, of all things!

©2009. Allyn & Bacon, a division of Pearson Education. Developed by Vicki Spandel. All rights reserved.

Revising with Informational Voice

Trait Connection: **Voice**

Introduction

Informational writing is formal, dry, and, let's face it—a bit dull. But then, that's how it's *supposed* to be, right? *Wrong!* Those are lies, actually. Big ones. The truth is, there are *no* dull topics, and *no* dull forms of writing. There *are* bored writers, however. And a bored writer kills off a little bit of voice with every sentence. If you choose a topic you care about in the first place, researching it should feel as exciting as shopping your favorite electronics store for a new gadget. You should feel that same sense of curiosity and anticipation. Let's say you buy something wonderful . . . you pick it out, but it's not *for* you. It's for someone else. You wrap it carefully, and then later, you have the fun of watching as the lucky person unwraps what you chose . . . slowly unveiling the surprise. Hold that feeling in your mind because it's the same feeling you get when writing works well. When you choose a good topic, it's like picking out a gift for your reader. You wrap it in your own voice, knowing how much fun the reader will have discovering the intriguing bits of information you carefully gathered in your research. That kind of writing is a gift from the heart.

Teacher's Sidebar . . .

In this lesson, students will be working on copy that is not their own—and so naturally, they will not have chosen the topics. They can still make a big difference in the voice of each piece, however. And the techniques they learn will make a big difference in their own writing—even *more so* when they have an opportunity to choose their own topics. It will help if you can provide relevant information on the topics, or allow students a *brief* amount of time for personal research. It need not be extensive. The point of this lesson is that good *informational* voice comes from (1) choosing a topic in which you have a strong interest, and (2) knowing that topic well.

Focus and Intent

This lesson is intended to help students:

- Appreciate the power of a strong informational voice.
- Practice writing with a sense of authority.
- Revise a short piece to strengthen informational voice.

Teaching the Lesson

Step 1: Sounding Fascinated

You know how catchy yawns are? One person starts . . . *and . . . then . . . oh, my . . . we're all doing it . . .* When informational writers sound as if they're about to fall asleep, readers start yawning and stretching, too. Hey—snap out of it. Rewrite each of the following informational tidbits to give it a bit of authority. Even if you don't know one thing about the topic, sound *fascinated*—it's contagious. And if you *do* have additional information to share, by all means do so. The first one is done for you—and by the way, you do *not* have to use quotations, but Paulsen's is a good fit, don't you think?

1. ***Yawn . . .***

   A moose sometimes behaves strangely. Moose can be dangerous.

   One more time, with *authority*—

   A moose is completely unpredictable—and because of its enormous size, one of the most dangerous animals on the planet. Gary Paulsen has compared the moose to a "deranged Chevy" (*Hatchet*. 2007. Simon & Schuster, p. 151).

2. ***Yawn . . .***

   Through the NASA space program, many discoveries are made which benefit us in our everyday lives, such as the development of robots.

   One more time, with *authority*—

   _____

   _____

3. ***Yawn . . .***

   As we make room for more shopping centers and housing developments, we need to also take time to think about the habitats of plants and animals we might be affecting.

   One more time, with *authority*—

   _____

   _____

Step 2: Making the Reading-Writing Connection

In his book *The Prairie Builders*, author Sneed B. Collard tells readers the history of America's great prairie lands, and urges a reawakening to spur preservation of this vanishing resource. In this paragraph, he tells of a restoration movement that began in the 1960s. The question is, was it too little too late? Notice the urgency in his voice. Is this writer sleepily feeding us statistics—or is he passionate about his topic?

By the early 1900s, more than 96 percent of America's tallgrass prairie had been turned into farms and grazing lands. In Iowa, the numbers were even more dramatic. Of the 36 million acres of prairie in Iowa, less than one tenth of one percent survived the plow. If you imagine that the original prairie was the size of a football field, all that remained was a little patch eight feet long and seven feet wide.

(From *The Prairie Builders* by Sneed B. Collard III. 2005. Boston: Houghton Mifflin. Page 11.)

Collard shares several statistics with us in this informational piece—and statistics can be difficult to remember. What strategy does this writer use to fix the impact of the loss in readers' minds? Does it work?

Step 3: Involving Students as Evaluators

Ask students to review Samples A and B, looking and listening for the enthusiasm, sense of authority, and engagement with the topic that produce voice in informational writing. Have students work with a partner, highlighting passionate moments, noting which piece is stronger in voice and asking how a writer might say the same thing differently to create *more* voice.

Discussing Results

Most students should identify Sample B as stronger. The writer of Sample A seems to simply be filling up the page. One possible revision of Sample A is provided.

Step 4: Modeling Revision

- If possible, provide students with a sample of a topographical map. Look at the lines, and talk about how a topographical map works to show elevation. Ask how such a map might be useful to hikers or fire fighters.

- Share Sample C (*Whole Class Revision*) with students. Read it aloud, listening for moments of strong informational voice: passion, excitement about the topic, sense of authority, engagement.

- Talk about whether the writer of Sample C has a strong informational voice. (Most students should say *no*.) Invite students to coach you through a class revision, first talking about the main point the writer is trying to make, and then brainstorming ways the writer could say the same thing with more voice.

- When you finish, read through the entire piece, listening for passion and a sense of authority. If you wish, compare your revision with ours, remembering that yours need not match ours in any way.

Step 5: Revising with Partners

Brainstorm things people can do to maintain aerobic fitness. Take a minute to show students how to calculate maximum heart rate for a workout: *Subtract your age from 220; then multiply that number by .8, or 80 percent.* When everyone understands how to do this, pass out copies of Sample D (*Revising with Partners*). Ask students to follow the basic steps you modeled with Sample C. *Working with partners,* they should:

- Read the piece aloud, listening for moments of voice.

- Talk about the writer's main message: What is he or she trying to convey to readers?

- Talk about ways to say the same thing with more passion and authority.

- (Optional) Research the topic online to identify one new bit of information to share. Interesting information strengthens voice.

- Revise the piece so that it has a stronger sense of authority—and reveals the writer's passion for the topic.

- Read the result aloud to hear the difference.

Step 6: Sharing and Discussing Results

When students have finished, ask several pairs of students to share their revisions aloud. Which revisions revealed the strongest voice? Did any teams do research to uncover new information on the topic? (Feel free to share our suggested revision, keeping in mind that students' revisions need not match ours in any way.)

Next Steps

- Invite students to revise their own informational writing, first reading it aloud to identify and highlight *three moments* where the voice could be stronger. They should begin by rewriting those three moments to say the same thing with more enthusiasm and sense of authority. Then, take it to the next step by researching the topic to uncover new bits of information that can pump life into their writing. The results will surprise them—and you.

- When students share informational writing in response groups, ask listeners to note on a 3×5 card *one standout moment* where the voice really grabs them, and turn all cards in to the writer. This tells the writer what is working, and is very useful in guiding revision.

- Listen and look for moments of voice in the informational writing you share aloud. Listen for enthusiasm, special knowledge of or fondness for a topic, personal commitment, passion, curiosity and fascination, and an eagerness to share bits of information not everyone knows. These are the marks of voice in informational writing. Recommended:

  - *The Prairie Builders* by Sneed B. Collard III. 2005. Boston: Houghton Mifflin. (This book epitomizes the power of personal research: Note that it was written *and photographed* by Sneed Collard, who has visited and studied the land he writes about. Other noteworthy touches include a glossary and list of recommended readings and relevant websites.)

- *The Dangerous Book for Boys* by Gonn Iggulden and Hal Iggulden. 2006. New York: HarperCollins. (These people *loved* writing this book, and their enthusiasm pops off every page.)

- *The Daring Book for Girls* by Andrea J. Buchanan and Miriam Peskowitz. 2007. New York: HarperCollins. (Topics from yoga to the periodic table are all presented with engagement and a sense of wonder.)

- *Hatchet: 25th Anniversary Edition* by Gary Paulsen. 2007. Boston: Houghton Mifflin. (Though this is not an informational piece per se, it is research-based. Note the sidebars—new to this edition—in which Paulsen shares an insider's perspective on how he gained the firsthand information that gives his text such irresistible authenticity.)

■ *For an additional challenge: The Dangerous Book for Boys* and *The Daring Book for Girls* are written essentially as guides to life. Why not create *The Daring Book for Writers*—and include some tips for putting voice into informational writing as well as other forms. After all, voice is all about danger and daring.

Sample A

Strong
Informational
Voice?

Cleopatra

Cleopatra is one of the most interesting people in history. She was born a very long time ago, in Egypt, where she became queen, and became very famous. Cleopatra grew up in Alexandria, which is a famous city in Egypt, known for a variety of things. Cleopatra may have been very beautiful, but no one knows for sure.

During her reign, Cleopatra knew other famous people, including Julius Caesar. Julius Caesar and Cleopatra had a child together. He did not live very long. Cleopatra herself later committed suicide.

Cleopatra is still well known today, and many films have been made about her amazing, fascinating life.

©2009. Allyn & Bacon, a division of Pearson Education. Developed by Vicki Spandel. All rights reserved.

Sample B

Strong
Informational
Voice?

Amelia Earhart

Amelia Earhart, born in 1897, is famous for her independent spirit, and for being the first woman to fly across the Atlantic—a feat for which she received the Distinguished Flying Cross. At an early age, she took her first ride in an airplane, and was immediately hooked. Shortly after, she purchased her own plane, which she named "The Canary," and declared she wanted to take lessons so she could fly by herself.

Fly by herself she did, racking up a whole series of "firsts": first woman to fly the Atlantic solo, first woman to fly coast-to-coast across the U.S. nonstop, and first person to fly solo across the Pacific—to name a few of her many achievements. She held numerous speed records, and was recognized by many as a crackerjack pilot (though not *all* historians agree on that). When she married G. P. Putnam (of Putnam Publishing), she chose to retain her own name, announcing that she did not care to be called "Mrs. Putnam"—or Mrs. *Anything*. She was Amelia Earhart. Period.

In 1937, Earhart attempted for the second time to fulfill her lifelong dream of circumnavigating the globe in a plane. She had completed 22,000 miles of the trip, and was headed over the Pacific to Howland Island—on the home stretch—when her plane went missing. Following months of intense searching, she was declared dead in 1939. People around the world grieved. Many historians believe her plane crashed into the ocean—but some think she landed on a remote atoll in the Pacific, where she clung to life for quite some time, hoping to be rescued. Fans are drawn to that story because it shows Amelia as they like to remember her: an adventurer and a fighter.

©2009. Allyn & Bacon, a division of Pearson Education. Developed by Vicki Spandel. All rights reserved.

Suggested Revision of Sample A

Cleopatra

Cleopatra ~~is~~ *was* one of the most ~~interesting people in history.~~ *powerful women in the world during her life.* She was born *in 70 BC* ~~a very long time ago,~~ in Egypt, where she became queen *when she was only 18, sharing the throne with her brother Ptolemy.* ~~and became~~

~~very famous.~~ Cleopatra grew up in Alexandria, ~~which is~~ a famous city in Egypt, known for ~~a variety of things.~~ *its incredible library, the largest in the world at that time.* Cleopatra *was of Greek descent, and* may have been very beautiful, but ~~no one knows~~ *who can say* for sure? *Standards of beauty change through the ages. There are numerous paintings of Cleopatra, but they are only products of the artists' imaginations.*

During her reign, Cleopatra ~~knew other~~ *sought power, and made it a point to meet* famous people, including Julius Caesar. Julius Caesar and Cleopatra had a child together, *named Caesarion.* He did not live very long. *Political enemies, fearing his power, had him executed at the age of 12.* Cleopatra herself later committed suicide. *As the story goes, she provoked a poisonous snake, called an asp, into biting her—and died both quickly and dramatically.*

Cleopatra is still well known today, and many films have been made about her amazing, fascinating life. *All feature her famous death scene. Though she lived only 40 years, that was enough to leave her mark on the world and her image on many coins.*

©2009. Allyn & Bacon, a division of Pearson Education. Developed by Vicki Spandel. All rights reserved.

Sample C: Whole Class Revision

Strong
Informational
Voice?

Topography

A topographical map is a very handy tool. A topographical map is a map that is covered with many wavy lines. The lines show elevation. If you trace one of the lines with your finger, you are moving along the same elevation. When lines are close together on the map, that shows that the terrain is rising steeply. When the lines are far apart on the map, that shows a gradual slope.

This kind of map is handy for hikers. It can tell them if the place they want to hike is steep or not. It can also be handy for fire fighters because when the terrain is very steep, it can be hard to move fire fighting equipment through it.

A topographical map is a good thing to have if you are planning a hike.

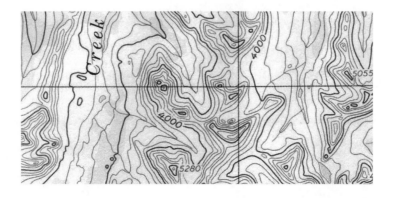

©2009. Allyn & Bacon, a division of Pearson Education. Developed by Vicki Spandel. All rights reserved.

Sample D: Revising with Partners

Strong Informational Voice?

Workout Routine

Most people do some kind of aerobic workout. They do not always know how hard to work, though. Here's a way to tell if you're working out hard enough. Subtract your age from the number 220. Then, calculate 80 percent of that number. The result is your maximum heart rate. You should still be able to carry on a conversation while you work out.

You can get to your maximum heart rate up by doing a number of different exercises. Do something you like to do. Do different things on different days. The important thing is to keep exercising.

The other important thing is how long it takes to get your heart rate back to normal. If it takes less than two minutes, you are in good shape. If it takes longer than four minutes, you might want to work out more.

©2009. Allyn & Bacon, a division of Pearson Education. Developed by Vicki Spandel. All rights reserved.

Suggested Revisions of C and D

Sample C: Whole Class Revision

What Those Squiggly Lines Really Mean

~~Topography~~

A topographical map is a very handy tool ~~A topographical~~ **especially for hikers or fire fighters.**

It's a different looking map ~~is a map that is~~ covered with many wavy lines. The **called topos.**

The ~~topos~~ **The more lines, the hillier the region.** lines show elevation. If you trace one of the ~~lines~~ with your

It's like walking along the side of a hill, not going up or down. finger, you are moving along the same elevation. When

lines are close together on the map, that shows that the

In that area, you might find yourself doing actual mountain climbing. terrain is rising steeply. When the lines are far apart on the

map, that shows a gradual slope.

This kind of map ~~is handy for hikers.~~ It can tell ~~them~~ **hikers**

about right for their skill level—or way too challenging. if the place they want to hike is ~~steep or not~~ It can ~~also be~~ **tell whether so**

~~handy for~~ fire fighters ~~because when~~ the terrain is ~~very~~

that they will find it impossible steep ~~it can be hard~~ to move fire fighting equipment through

it. **The map may also help them spot an alternate route for getting to the fire.**

~~A topographical map is a good thing to have if you~~

~~are planning a hike.~~ **Don't even think about hiking without a topographical map tucked into your pocket. It could save you from climbing a granite wall when you only meant to hike the meadow!**

©2009. Allyn & Bacon, a division of Pearson Education. Developed by Vicki Spandel. All rights reserved.

Sample D: Revising with Partners

Being Good to Your Heart

~~Workout Routine~~

these days   often don't know

Most people do some kind of aerobic workout. They ~~do not always know~~

if they're working hard enough,   an easy

~~how hard to work~~ though. Here's a way to tell   ~~if you're working out hard~~

Let's say you were 20. The result would be 220 minus 20, or 200.

~~enough.~~ Subtract your age from the number 220. Then, calculate 80 percent

Eighty percent of 200 is 160, the maximum
heart rate for someone 20 years old.

of that number. The result is your maximum heart rate. You should still be

able to carry on a conversation while you work out. That's another quick

and easy way to check whether you are working too hard.

You can get to your maximum heart rate up by doing a number of

so   love: swim, bike, ski, jog, or roller skate.

different exercises do something you ~~like to do~~ Do different things on

so you don't get bored. If you're bored, you might quit!

different days. The important thing is to keep exercising for at least

half an hour, and face it—an hour is better!

Pay very close attention to

~~The other important thing is~~ how long it takes to get your heart rate

superb

back to normal. If it takes less than two minutes, you are in ~~good~~ shape. If

need to get serious about working out. Come on. Be good to your heart!

it takes longer than four minutes, you ~~might want to work out more~~

©2009. Allyn & Bacon, a division of Pearson Education. Developed by Vicki Spandel. All rights reserved.

Putting It Together
(Editing Lessons 10, 12, and 14)

Trait Connection: **Conventions**

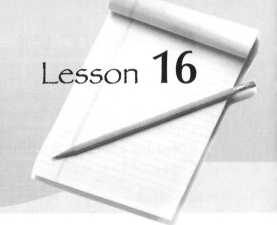

Introduction (Share with students in your own words.)

In this lesson, you will have a chance to put skills from three editing lessons together. You will

- Add dashes for emphasis, or to point out something important: *Zach broiled three steaks—but ate none of them.*

- Use parentheses to set off nonessential information (as if whispering to the reader): *It was forty below zero (Fahrenheit).*

- Use ellipses to create a dramatic pause in the text: *The dark figure crept closer . . . and closer.* OR, *"Wait . . . let me think . . . her name was Esmeralda!" Rose recalled with a triumphant grin.*

In this lesson, you'll have opportunities to use all these marks of punctuation—but you will need to use your own editor's judgment to decide when each mark is appropriate. There are no hard and fast right or wrong answers, though we will offer suggestions. Look for two opportunities to use a dash, two to use parentheses, and two to use ellipsis.

Teaching the Lesson (General Guidelines for Teachers)

1. Begin by reviewing the concepts: use of dashes, use of parentheses, and use of ellipses. Make sure all three punctuation marks are clear in students' minds.

2. Answer any questions students may have. You may want students to have printouts of the edited copy from Lessons 10, 12, and 14 in front of them. It is fine for them to refer to these lessons as they work. This is practice, not a test.

3. Share the editing lesson on the following page. Students should read the passage aloud, looking *and listening* for things they wish to change.

4. Ask them to work individually first, then check with a partner.

5. When everyone is done, ask them to coach you as you edit the same copy, making any changes you and they decide are important.

6. When you finish, compare your edited copy to the one on page 141.

7. Remember that you must use your own judgment—and your final decisions may differ from what is shown on our edited copy. That is fine, so long as your final draft reads smoothly and you can defend your decisions.

Editing Goals: Use dashes, parentheses, and ellipses to create readable copy.

Editing Practice

Consider 2 dashes.
Consider 2 sets of parentheses.
Consider 2 ellipses.

"What time do you have ?" Chuck asked, peering at his own watch which had stopped dead.

"I can't quite make it out it's about 3:02," said Lucien, looking closely. The minute hand on his watch was broken. "Wait. That can't be right," he added. "It's actually 12:15 or no, make that *12:16* actually."

Chuck grew visibly annoyed. "Don't you have *any* sense of time?" he asked, still staring at his own watch. It seemed to Chuck that Lucien Chuck's brother had been late for one thing or another all his life. "You need a new watch!" he said.

"I like *this* one," Lucien responded. "Someone gave it to me you!" Chuck had to smile. They headed home at 12:17.

©2009. Allyn & Bacon, a division of Pearson Education. Developed by Vicki Spandel. All rights reserved.

Edited Copy

2 dashes (lines 2 and 13)
2 sets of parentheses (lines 9 and 13–14)
2 ellipses (lines 3 and 6)

"What time do you have ?" Chuck asked, peering at his own watch—which had stopped dead.

"I can't quite make it out . . . it's about 3:02," said Lucien, looking closely. The minute hand on his watch was broken. "Wait. That can't be right," he added. "It's actually 12:15 . . . or no, make that *12:16,* actually."

Chuck grew visibly annoyed. "Don't you have *any* sense of time?" he asked, still staring at his own watch. It seemed to Chuck that Lucien (Chuck's brother) had been late for one thing or another all his life. "You need a new watch!" he said.

"I like *this* one," Lucien responded. "Someone gave it to me—you!" Chuck had to smile. They headed home (at 12:17).

©2009. Allyn & Bacon, a division of Pearson Education. Developed by Vicki Spandel. All rights reserved.

Revising a Complaint Letter

Trait Connection: **Voice**

Introduction

Quick—think of a synonym for *complain.* Did you think of any or *all* of these—*criticize, gripe, grumble, nitpick, fume, whine,* or *nag?* If so, you just figured out seven things NOT to do in a complaint letter. A complaint letter isn't really about *complaining*—it's about offering a helpful suggestion. Maybe we should call it the Helpful Suggestion Letter. Not as catchy, but more accurate. In such a letter, tone of voice is everything. Remember the last time someone whined at *you?* Remember how cooperative that made you feel? *Right.* Save your whiny voice for when you just want to be annoying—like a mosquito. For this lesson, pull out one of the most powerful weapons a writer can have: the helpful voice of someone with a *really good* suggestion to offer, if someone will *just listen . . .*

Teacher's Sidebar . . .

The quality of a writer's voice is measured not only by *how much* voice he or she puts into the writing, but also by whether it's the *right voice* for the moment. In the case of a complaint letter—or any letter, really—the right voice is achieved by imagining how it feels to be the recipient, and what it would take to get that person to respond in a favorable way. Although the focus of this lesson is on voice, notice that an amicable, friendly, supportive voice is achieved partly through word choice.

Focus and Intent

This lesson is intended to help students:

- Appreciate the power of a friendly, supportive voice.
- Recognize the "right" voice for a complaint letter that is meant to *get results,* not just sound off.
- Revise a hostile, confrontational letter to give it a more appropriate and effective voice.

Teaching the Lesson

Step 1: Getting the Reader to Listen

Sometimes, when we are criticized, we respond the way most people do in an uncomfortable situation. We tune out, and take our minds elsewhere. That is the very *last thing* you want when you're trying to get someone to respond to your very real needs. Following are some confrontational moments from complaint letters. Ask yourself how *you would feel* if these words were directed toward you. Would you listen—or tune out? Then, revise the wording to make the voice more friendly—a voice to which your reader will listen and respond. The first one is done for you.

Sample 1
Complaining voice

I don't know what you people were thinking when you published this book, but it certainly won't be of any interest to readers my age.

Friendlier voice

Though the cover suggests that this book might be appropriate for sixth graders, I feel you'd have more success marketing it to younger readers.

Sample 2
Complaining voice

Do you guys ever try eating the food from your own restaurant? Give me a break! You couldn't choke down one of these burgers even with a gallon of ketchup.

Friendlier voice

_____

_____

Sample 3
Complaining voice

Last week some friends and I tried to play Frisbee in the city park, but there was so much trash, we couldn't move without tripping over it. Why don't you <u>do</u> something? It's disgusting! We won't be back until you clean up your act.

Friendlier voice

_____

_____

Step 2: Making the Reading-Writing Connection

Several years ago, a student named Henry wrote a complaint letter to a local candy company. His complaint was simple: he didn't think it fair that some packages of candy contained more pieces than others. Here's a small excerpt from his letter. If you were president of the candy company, would he get a positive response from you?

Your candy is delicious. I eat it all the time. However, did you know that some packages contain more pieces of candy than others? I am sure you did not mean for this to happen, but it does not seem fair. After all, every package costs exactly the same. Could you please check this out?

Would you guess Henry got a response? If you said *yes*, you're right. The candy company wrote a very cordial letter back, thanking Henry for his comments—and also sent a whole case of individual candy packages, enough to share with everyone in his class. Henry not only got the attention of the candy company, but he made his classmates pretty happy, too.

Step 3: Involving Students as Evaluators

Ask students to review Samples A and B, looking and listening for the tone of voice that each writer projects in his or her letter of complaint. Have students work with a partner, highlighting moments they feel are inappropriate or confrontational (even hostile), and thinking about how the writer might say the same thing differently, with a more appropriate voice.

Discussing Results

Most students should identify Sample B as more appropriate—and more likely to get a positive response. The writer of Sample A is highly confrontational. This kind of rhetoric *may* get a response—but the dialogue is off to a poor start! One possible revision of Sample A is provided.

Step 4: Modeling Revision

- Share Sample C (*Whole Class Revision*) with students. Read it aloud, listening carefully to the tone of voice. Is it respectful, courteous, and friendly? Or confrontational and angry?

- Talk about whether the writer of Sample C has used the appropriate voice for this type of letter, a voice that will prompt a positive response. (Most students should say *no*.) Invite students to coach you through a class revision, first identifying and highlighting angry moments, then revising by deleting some copy or toning down the rhetoric.

- When you finish, read through the entire piece, listening for a friendly voice that will elicit a positive response. If you wish, compare your revision with ours, remembering that yours need not match ours in any way.

Step 5: Revising with Partners

Share copies of Sample D (*Revising with Partners*). Ask students to follow the basic steps you modeled with Sample C. *Working with partners,* they should:

- Read the piece aloud, listening carefully to the voice, and asking whether it is appropriate, and whether it is likely to get a positive response.

- Highlight words or phrases that seem hostile, angry, or confrontational.

- Revise each hostile moment by either deleting copy or rewording to give it a softer, friendlier tone.

- Read the result aloud to hear the difference in voice.

144

Step 6: Sharing and Discussing Results

When students have finished, ask several pairs of students to share their revisions aloud. Did teams tend to target the same passages for revision? Which team(s) found the most positive ways to express their feelings or needs? (Feel free to share our suggested revision, keeping in mind that students' revisions need not match ours in any way.)

Next Steps

- Consider writing actual letters to businesses in your community. They need not be letters of complaint. Letters praising a company for its products or services are always welcome, and provide good practice for achieving the right voice in a business letter.

- Create a class list of tips for writing a good complaint letter—or business letter of any kind. Don't forget (in addition to issues of voice) such little things as stating your need or question plainly, and including important relevant information (names, dates, times, etc.).

- Students who like to communicate via email may enjoy writing to someone famous. It is important to remember that the same attention to clarity, good conventions, and a positive tone of voice apply—if writers wish to receive a positive response. The current president can be contacted at president@whitehouse.gov For email addresses of many other well-known persons in many walks of life, check out the book *E-Mail Addresses of the Rich and Famous* by Seth Godin (1997, Addison-Wesley/Longman), or simply search under "email addresses for famous people" online.

- In this technology-happy time, handwritten notes are a rarity—but many people treasure them. Consider designing and writing your own greeting cards for an audience who will deeply appreciate them: parents or grandparents, younger children, hospital patients or nursing home residents, military personnel—or any audience of your choice.

- Letter writing of all kinds is a wonderful way to develop voice because the audience is built in. Many students enjoy writing to teachers, and may like to hear samples of letters adults have written to teachers they still remember. For such examples, see:

  - *Letters to My Teacher: Tributes to the People Who Have Made a Difference.* Edited by Barb Karg and Rick Sutherland. 2006. Avon, MA: Adams Media.

- *For an additional challenge:* Many writers (and illustrators) love receiving fan mail from student readers—and often write back. Invite students to write letters to favorite authors, and to share their letters and responses with the class. You can simply type in "letters to authors" online for several sites. Or check out www.superkidz.com/authors for Ms. Kilroy's "Authors and Illustrators of the Week."

Sample A: Email to A-1 Sporting Goods

Dear A-1 Sporting Goods:

The right voice? Friendly or adversarial?

What on earth were you trying to do, kill me??!! Yesterday I rented snow shoes from your pathetic store. This has to have been one of the worst experiences of my whole life! The straps came apart when I was up to my knees in snow, and this was a very hard problem to fix! I could have easily broken my leg! Do you even care about your customers at all?

I suggest that you take five minutes to inspect your equipment before you rent it out to poor unsuspecting customers such as myself. I demand my money back!

Sincerely,

Tom

©2009. Allyn & Bacon, a division of Pearson Education. Developed by Vicki Spandel. All rights reserved.

Sample B: Email to Lazy Day

The right voice?
Friendly or
adversarial?

Dear Lazy Day Picnic Company:

My friends and I have bought food from your store many times, and it has always been very good. Last night, though, something strange happened.

We ordered fried chicken, pizza, and macaroni salad for our end-of-season soccer game. I think we must have gotten someone else's order by mistake. We received deviled eggs and ham sandwiches—but only enough for two people, and there were twenty of us! Do you think those two people got *our* picnic? If so, they must have been pretty full—but I bet they did not complain!

We realize that providing us with another whole picnic would be expensive, but we have spent a lot of money for food we did not get—and by the time we figured out what had happened, your store was closed for the night. Now our soccer season is over. Can you suggest a way of making everyone happy? We are hoping to order next year's picnic from you, too!

Best wishes,

Becca

©2009. Allyn & Bacon, a division of Pearson Education. Developed by Vicki Spandel. All rights reserved.

Suggested Revision of Sample A

Dear A-1 Sporting Goods:

~~What on earth were you trying to do, kill me??!!~~

Yesterday I rented snow shoes from your ~~pathetic~~ store.
Unfortunately, I had some trouble with them.
^ ~~This has to have been one of the worst experiences of my~~

~~whole life!~~ The straps came apart when I was up to my

knees in snow, and this was a very hard problem to fix!
Luckily, I was not injured.
^ ~~I could have easily broken my leg! Do you even care about~~

~~your customers at all?~~ **I am sure you would never knowingly
rent equipment that was unsafe.**

Is it possible that my pair of show shoes had not been inspected?
^ ~~I suggest that you take five minutes to inspect your~~

~~equipment before you rent it out to poor unsuspecting~~

~~customers such as myself. I demand my money back!~~
**I feel the fair thing to do would be to refund my
money for the rental, or to give me free rental on a
sound, carefully inspected pair of show shoes. I hope
you agree!**

Sincerely,

Tom

©2009. Allyn & Bacon, a division of Pearson Education. Developed by Vicki Spandel. All rights reserved.

Sample C: Whole Class Revision

> The right voice? Friendly or adversarial?

Dear Voyageur Touring Company:

I don't know if you recall, but our sixth grade class did a field trip to your company just last week. For the most part, it was interesting, but I have some suggestions to share with you.

First of all, we could not hear the tour guide. Why don't you tell people to speak up when they are doing a guided tour? I missed *most* of what our guide said.

Second, excuse me for saying so, but field trips where you don't get to actually DO anything are really boring. You could have let us climb into a canoe or look through binoculars or something! Just standing around listening to someone talk is not my idea of fun.

Have a good summer,

Naomi

©2009. Allyn & Bacon, a division of Pearson Education. Developed by Vicki Spandel. All rights reserved.

Sample D: Revising with Partners

Dear Quick-Speak:

I bought your set of CDs that promised to teach

me to speak French in three months or less. Well, guess what. It has

been more than four months, and I still do not speak French! This

program obviously does not work! It is worthless!

Your ad promises that I can have my money back if the program

does not work for me. I think you should give me every cent of it. Your

program is a total joke and I would never recommend it to my friends. As

soon as you send my money, I am going to start saving for a trip to Paris.

Good luck,

Robert

> The right voice?
> Friendly or
> adversarial?

©2009. Allyn & Bacon, a division of Pearson Education. Developed by Vicki Spandel. All rights reserved.

Suggested Revisions of C and D

Sample C: Whole Class Revision

Dear Voyageur Touring Company:

~~I don't know if you recall, but~~ Thank you for inviting our sixth grade class ~~did a field trip~~ on a field trip of ~~to~~ your company ~~just~~ last week. ~~For the most part, it~~ The whole experience was interesting, ~~but~~ and I have some suggestions ~~to share with you.~~ to make it even better!

First of all, ~~we~~ you probably don't realize this, but many of us could not hear the tour guide. ~~Why don't you tell~~ It could be helpful to provide a microphone or just remind people to speak up when they are doing a guided tour. Because I missed *most* of what our guide said, I wonder if you could send me a brochure about your company.

Second, ~~excuse me for saying so, but~~ field trips ~~where you don't get to actually DO anything are really boring.~~ are even more interesting when people get to actually DO things. You ~~could have let us~~ might consider inviting students to climb into a canoe or look through binoculars. ~~or something! Just standing around listening to someone talk is not my idea of fun.~~ Think what a hit your field trips would be then!

Thanks again and have a good summer,

Naomi

©2009. Allyn & Bacon, a division of Pearson Education. Developed by Vicki Spandel. All rights reserved.

Sample D: Revising with Partners

Dear Quick-Speak:

I bought your set of CDs that promised to teach me to speak

[I have worked very hard on the program for]

French in three months or less. ~~Well, guess what. It has been~~ more than

[am sorry to say that I]

four months, and I still do not speak French! This ~~program obviously~~

[is very disappointing, when your program seemed like such a good one.]

~~does not work! It is worthless!~~

Your ad promises that I can have my money back if the program

[hope you will honor this promise
and refund the full price of $50.]   Although

does not work for me. I ~~think you should give me every cent of it~~ Your

[did not work for me, others might have more luck with it.]

program ~~is a total joke and I would never recommend it to my friends. As~~

[As you can see, I am returning the CDs in good condition. Can I expect my
refund this week? Thank you, and good luck with your future programs!]

~~soon as you send my money, I am going to start saving for a trip to Paris.~~

Sincerely,
~~Good luck~~

Robert

©2009. Allyn & Bacon, a division of Pearson Education. Developed by Vicki Spandel. All rights reserved.

You May Quote Me

Trait Connection: **Conventions**

Introduction (Share with students in your own words.)

Quotation marks set off a speaker's exact words—just the way a bubble does in a comic strip. If it doesn't fall *inside* the quotation marks, the reader assumes the speaker didn't *say* it. This is important—because we want the right person to get credit for speaking, and we want to know precisely what the person said. Quotation marks are handy when you want to insert a comment into a report, as in the following example. Notice that title, author, year, publisher, and page number are *all* provided for the reader—who can now look up this quotation for him- or herself:

> Amelia Earhart has been quoted as saying, "Adventure is worthwhile in itself." (Andrea J. Buchanan and Miriam Peskowitz, *The Daring Book for Girls*. 2007. HarperCollins. Page 278.)

Every time you quote someone else (as opposed to making things up yourself), you need to cite the source. It's a courtesy to the person whose words you are quoting, but also to the reader, who might love that quotation so much that he or she wants to check out the source personally.

Quotation marks are also used to set off speech in dialogue—which is what we'll consider in this lesson. Here are a couple of things to keep in mind. First, make sure you use the quotation marks in pairs: one set to start the speech, one to close it off. Second, put commas and periods *that are part of the speech* inside the quotation marks. Which one you use depends on how the speech is set up:

> "Hand over my thesaurus," said Rose.

> Rose demanded, "Hand over my thesaurus."

In the first example, Rose's comment opens with what she says, and ends with the words *said Rose*. There is a comma (and not a period) after what Rose says because although her speech ends with the word *thesaurus*, the sentence does not end until the word *Rose*.

In the second example, Rose is identified first, and her comment comes second. In this case, the sentence and the comment end together. That is why there is a period after the word *thesaurus:* end of comment AND end of sentence. Notice that in the first sentence, the comma that goes with what Rose says comes *inside* the quotation marks. Similarly, in the second sentence, the period that goes with what Rose said comes *inside* the quotation marks.

Just to make sure all this placement of commas and periods and quotation marks is clear, let's try a little warm-up, bringing in another character, Gavin, just to make things more interesting.

Insert quotation marks using an upside down caret, like this: ⌄⌄ ⌄⌄
Insert a period with a large dot (you can circle it if you wish, as editors do): ⊙
Insert a comma with a caret, tucking the comma inside: ∧

Ready? OK—here we go:

> Rose said Hand over my thesaurus
>
> I'll never give it back Gavin replied

Your edited copy should look like this:

> Rose said,"Hand over my thesaurus⊙"
>
> "I'll never give it back,"Gavin replied⊙

How did you do? In the practice that follows, Rose and Gavin will continue their conversation. You will only need to insert three kinds of punctuation: commas, periods, and quotation marks. The paragraphing is done for you (we'll work on that later). You won't need exclamation points or question marks. (Those crafty little rascals pop up in the next lesson.) All the capitalization is correct as is, so don't worry about that either. *Periods, commas, quotation marks*—that's it. Notice that we have left extra spacing to make it easier for you to insert the punctuation you need. Keep the previous examples with Rose and Gavin at your elbow as you work.

Teaching the Lesson (General Guidelines for Teachers)

1. Share the examples above, or make up your own examples to practice punctuating dialogue by inserting commas, periods, and quotation marks in the appropriate places.

2. Encourage students to keep examples handy and refer to them often as they work through this lesson.

3. Share the editing lesson on the following page. Students should read the passage silently and aloud, looking and listening for actual speech, and thinking how best to punctuate it to make it clear.

4. Ask them to edit individually first, then check with a partner. Partners should practice reading aloud (softly) to each other.

5. When everyone is done, ask them to coach you as you edit the same copy.

6. When you finish, read your edited copy aloud, taking time to point out which portions are actual speech, and to indicate why commas or periods are appropriate in various spots. Compare your edited copy with our suggested text on page 157.

Editing Goal: Punctuate dialogue correctly.
Follow-Up: Review dialogue in your own writing to make sure it is punctuated correctly. Also make sure you have used quotation marks to set off any borrowed material, and that you have cited your source correctly.

Editing Practice

Punctuate dialogue using
- **Quotation marks**
- **Commas**
- **Periods**

Let's have some tea and talk things over said Rose

I'm not especially fond of tea Gavin answered

Rose said Try one cup before you make up your mind

If you don't mind, I'd rather not Gavin replied

Rose said Suit yourself, but at least return my thesaurus

Gavin answered Not on your life

You're a thief then Rose said

Gavin replied I might be a thief, but at least I'm not a tea drinker

True Rose admitted

©2009. Allyn & Bacon, a division of Pearson Education. Developed by Vicki Spandel. All rights reserved.

Edited Copy

Nine lines of dialogue punctuated, using periods, commas, and quotation marks

"Let's have some tea and talk things over," said Rose.

"I'm not especially fond of tea," Gavin answered.

Rose said, "Try one cup before you make up your mind."

"If you don't mind, I'd rather not," Gavin replied.

Rose said, "Suit yourself, but at least return my thesaurus."

Gavin answered, "Not on your life."

"You're a thief then," Rose said.

Gavin replied, "I might be a thief, but at least I'm not a tea drinker."

"True," Rose admitted.

©2009. Allyn & Bacon, a division of Pearson Education. Developed by Vicki Spandel. All rights reserved.

Revising with Descriptive Clout

Trait Connection: **Word Choice**

Introduction

Good writers are choosy about adjectives. First, they don't overdo it. They don't write about "breathtaking, gorgeous, spectacular mountains" when "majestic mountains" will do. They also avoid words that say nothing specific: *great, nice, wonderful, awesome*. There is nothing *wrong* with these words. They just don't have the descriptive clout of more specific adjectives: *ferocious, delicate, scrawny, ravenous*. Precise words create sensory responses in a reader's mind. Sometimes, the best choices are words we might not first expect. In *Peter and the Starcatchers*, we're introduced to the governess, Mrs. Bumbrake, this way: "The girl stood next to a stout woman, wearing a wide-ranging and complicated skirt and wielding a formidable black umbrella" (Dave Barry and Ridley Pearson, 2004. Hyperion Books, page 20). *Wide-ranging* and *complicated* might not be the first words you'd think of to describe a skirt—and have you ever thought of an umbrella as *formidable?* Probably not—but readers *love* surprises. They also appreciate comparisons. These same writers later compare pirate Black Stache's nose to a "prize turnip" (p. 33). If you've ever seen a turnip, you get the picture.

Teacher's Sidebar . . .

In this lesson, students will revise by using four strategies: (1) deleting adjectives when there are *too many*, (2) replacing *weak* adjectives with stronger ones, (3) searching for adjectives that *surprise* the reader or create *vivid sensory impressions* in the mind, and (4) using comparisons: *She stood straight as a flagpole,* or *His hairy feet shuffled across the floor like rats in a very slow race.* You can do two things to help make this lesson successful: First, make sure your students know what an adjective is, and can identify adjectives in a sentence; and second, provide dictionaries or thesauruses to make exploration of choices easier.

Focus and Intent

This lesson is intended to help students:

- Appreciate the power of good description.
- Recognize several strategies for making description strong.
- Revise a weak descriptive piece to create vivid pictures in the reader's mind.

Teaching the Lesson

Step 1: Exploring Options

Following are several descriptions that are not as powerful or vivid as they might be. For each one, identify the adjectives. Then, revise by using *one or more* of these strategies: (1) delete superfluous adjectives, (2) replace general descriptions (*big*) with something more specific (*towering*), (3) use an unexpected word instead of the first word that comes to mind (*exploding* eyebrows instead of *bushy* eyebrows), or (4) use a comparison—*hands like lobster claws*. The first one is done for you.

Sample 1
Weak description
Ms. Pearl was a <u>nice</u> teacher with a <u>big</u> smile.

Stronger
Ms. Pearl was a <u>wise and perceptive</u> teacher with a <u>smile that spread across her whole face like morning sun</u>.

Sample 2
Weak description
The fisherman wore an old jacket. He had small eyes. He carried an unusual fishing net.

Stronger

_____

Sample 3
Weak description
Heavy rain hit the roof. It was loud. It was a wild, wacky, vicious storm.

Stronger

_____

Sample 4
Weak description
Our ride on the Ferris wheel was awesome and special. From the top, we could see the buildings of the city, looking small in the distance.

Stronger

_____

Step 2: Making the Reading-Writing Connection

The ant lion is an insect that preys on ants—hence its name. In the adult stage, it is fairly innocuous, floating in the air from leaf to leaf, looking—as author Bruce Brooks tells us, "merely decorative." In the larva stage, however, the ant lion is a ferocious hunter, burying most of its tiny, round body into the earth, so that only its claws protrude, awaiting an unsuspecting ant. How many different descriptive techniques does Brooks use in this passage? Keep in mind that the creature he is describing is scarcely bigger than the ant it preys upon:

159

The larva . . . looks as if it's right out of the next alien scare movie. It has the usual low-slung, wiggly larva body, and inadequate legs that seem barely able to keep its bulbous sac off the ground. But up front, on the head, loom a jagged set of pincers, clearly designed for sharp, crushing snatches. It's as if the little bug had somehow managed to swallow a much larger crab, and everything had gone down except one fierce claw left sticking out.

(From Bruce Brooks. *Predator!* 1991. New York: Farrar, Straus, and Giroux. Pages 14, 16.)

Do certain adjectives seem *just right* in this passage? Are any surprising? Does Brooks use any comparisons? What if Brooks had simply written, "The ant lion larva is a scary little bug with sharp claws." That would be accurate—but would it be effective?

Step 3: Involving Students as Evaluators

Ask students to review Samples A and B, looking and listening for moments of description. Have students work with a partner, highlighting adjectives and thinking about which ones work well and which could use some help.

Discussing Results

Most students should identify Sample A as the stronger piece. Sample B has too many adjectives—and most of them are too general to create any vivid impression. One possible revision of Sample B is provided.

Step 4: Modeling Revision

- Share Sample C (*Whole Class Revision*) with students. Read it aloud, listening carefully to the description.

- Talk about whether the writer of Sample C has been choosy enough about adjectives. Are they vivid—and sometimes unexpected? Do they create vivid sensory responses in the reader's mind? (Most students should say *no*.) Invite students to coach you through a class revision, first identifying and highlighting adjectives, then revising by using one or more of the four strategies emphasized in this lesson: (1) delete superfluous adjectives, (2) replace general descriptive words with something stronger, (3) reach for an unusual, unexpected adjective to surprise the reader, or (4) replace the adjective with a comparison.

- When you finish, read through the entire piece, asking students to close their eyes so they can test the power of the sensory impressions. If you wish, compare your revision with ours, remembering that yours need not match ours in any way.

Step 5: Revising with Partners

Share copies of Sample D (*Revising with Partners*). Ask students to follow the basic steps you modeled with Sample C. *Working with partners,* they should:

- Read the piece aloud, listening carefully to descriptive moments, and asking whether they are weak—or have some clout.

- Highlight all adjectives.
- Revise any descriptive moments that could be stronger by using one or more of the four strategies emphasized in this lesson.
- Read the result aloud to hear the difference in descriptive power.

Step 6: Sharing and Discussing Results

When students have finished, ask several pairs of students to share their revisions aloud. Did teams revise the same passages? Did they use the same or different strategies? (Feel free to share our suggested revision, keeping in mind that students' revisions need not match ours in any way.)

Next Steps

- Ask students to review their own work, both fiction and nonfiction, for descriptive moments, and to highlight any adjectives they have used. Ask them to consider revising one or more passages, using any of the strategies discussed in this lesson.

- When students meet in response groups, invite listeners to identify one descriptive moment that they find especially vivid, note it on a 3×5 card, and give it to the writer. This feedback is useful in helping writers identify the kinds of description that are working well.

- As a class, study something *alive*—bird, insect, reptile, spider, etc. Your subject can be on film, but a live model works best. Ask students, in pairs, to brainstorm adjectives and comparisons that effectively describe your subject. Make a list of the most effective descriptions.

- Try the same activity based on photographs—postcards work well for this exercise. After each person has made a list of five or more descriptive words and phrases, try matching descriptions to the photos that inspired them. If you can do it, you know the descriptions are vivid.

- Listen for effective descriptive writing in the literature you share with students. Don't forget to include nonfiction. Recommended:
  - *Predator!* by Bruce Brooks. 1991. New York: Farrar, Straus, and Giroux.
  - *Buzz: The Intimate Bond Between Humans and Insects* by Josie Glausiusz and Volker Steger. 2004. San Francisco: Chronicle Books.
  - *The Invention of Hugo Cabret* by Brian Selznick. 2007. New York: Scholastic. (Note that some of this unusual tale is told through drawings—many of which provide a good basis for descriptive writing.)
  - *Nature by Design* by Bruce Brooks. 1991. New York: Farrar, Straus, and Giroux.
  - *The Schwa Was Here* by Neal Shusterman. 2004. New York: Puffin Books.

- *For an additional challenge:* Try writing a descriptive piece without using *any* adjectives. This requires careful attention to precise nouns and energetic verbs, plus some talent for making striking comparisons.

Sample A

Strong
description?
Anything to
cut or change?

The mountains rose like great silver crystals poking up from the earth. Hans and I had climbed an unforgiving trail with precipitous drop-offs on one side, and now leaned against a welcoming rock to catch our breath. Before us an expansive meadow stretched out to a stubby line of firs we judged to be two miles from where we stood. We were tired, but we knew we would make it now. Hans grinned, pushing the fur-trimmed hood back from his ruddy face, calculating the time to sundown. Not long. A determined wind clawed at our cheeks. "Better get at it," he said, knowing that if we waited too long, one of us would fall asleep.

"You first," I told him, trying to coax some feeling into my numb toes. Hans took off ahead of me, his size 13 boots breaking trail through a fragile crust of frozen snow. I followed a good ten yards behind, watching Hans's thin frame aim for the trees like an unwavering compass needle.

©2009. Allyn & Bacon, a division of Pearson Education. Developed by Vicki Spandel. All rights reserved.

Sample B

Strong
description?
Anything to
cut or change?

The gorilla is an amazing animal. It is small and

tiny when it is born, usually weighing only four or

five pounds. But the male can grow to a huge, immense

weight of five hundred pounds—all muscle!

This animal is special for many reasons. First, it has

an amazing way of walking: on its knuckles! The gorilla

can stand on its hind legs, but chooses not to because its

arms are so strong, powerful, and muscular.

The gorilla is also a wonderful parent. Even the giant

silverbacks, the biggest of the males, are nice to the infant

gorillas. They play with them, and are not mean or vicious.

Mother gorillas are also nice, and allow the babies to ride

on their backs when they get tired.

Finally, the intelligence of the gorilla is awesome.

Gorillas use tools with great skill. They communicate with

each other in interesting ways, with a range of sounds and

gestures. No wonder humans consider this creature special.

©2009. Allyn & Bacon, a division of Pearson Education. Developed by Vicki Spandel. All rights reserved.

Suggested Revision of Sample B

a complex, social
The gorilla is ~~an amazing~~ animal. It ~~is small and tiny when it is born,~~

(weighs less than a small cat at birth,)
~~usually weighing only four or five pounds,~~ but the male can grow to

an unbelievable
~~a huge, immense~~ weight of five hundred pounds—all muscle!

(intriguing to zoologists and animal lovers)   a curious
This animal is ~~special~~ for many reasons. First, it has ~~an amazing~~

way of walking: on its knuckles! The gorilla *can* stand on its hind legs, but

far more
chooses not to because its arms are ~~so strong~~ powerful. ~~and muscular,~~

loving
The gorilla is also a ~~wonderful~~ parent. Even the giant silverbacks,

gentle with
the biggest of the males, are ~~nice to~~ the infant gorillas. They play with

(as carefully as a human might handle a small bird.)   patient,
them ~~and are not mean or vicious,~~ Mother gorillas are also ~~nice~~ and

allow the babies to ride on their backs when they get tired.

impressive.
Finally, the intelligence of the gorilla is ~~awesome,~~ Gorillas use

(striking ingenuity, using rocks to crack open nuts.)
tools with ~~great skill,~~ They communicate with each other in ~~interesting~~

elaborate
ways, with a range of sounds and gestures. No wonder humans consider

as mesmerizing as any performer onstage.
this creature ~~special,~~

©2009. Allyn & Bacon, a division of Pearson Education. Developed by Vicki Spandel. All rights reserved.

Sample C: Whole Class Revision

Strong description? Anything to cut or change?

Snowboarding is a really cool sport. It's a lot like surfing, except it's done on snow instead of water. I don't know—there is just something amazing about zigzagging down a steep hill at 40 miles per hour. What a rush! The feeling when the board suddenly leaps into the air is amazing, incredible, and completely freeing.

It's really neat to watch expert snowboarders at work, taking amazing chances. They are just awesome.

After a day on the slopes, it feels nice and relaxing to just kick back and think about all the close calls. It's great to know you did something challenging and came through it OK.

©2009. Allyn & Bacon, a division of Pearson Education. Developed by Vicki Spandel. All rights reserved.

Sample D: Revising with Partners

Strong
description?
Anything to
cut or change?

Did you know that some people eat raw oysters?

To people who have never tried it, that might sound

yucky. Or downright gross. For them, it just isn't something

nice people do.

On the other hand, some people think oysters—raw

or not—are great! They think they're even better with a

spicy sauce or yummy slice of lemon.

It's true, oysters look a little weird. They look greasy,

oily, slippery, and slick. Oysters can feel a little nasty on

your tongue. Swallowing them can be an unusual

experience. But people who eat them often say that the

special thing about oysters is that with every bite, you get

the flavor of the sea itself. How amazing is that? Raw or

roasted, oysters definitely make for a special meal!

©2009. Allyn & Bacon, a division of Pearson Education. Developed by Vicki Spandel. All rights reserved.

Suggested Revisions of C and D

Sample C: Whole Class Revision

Snowboarding ~~is a really cool sport~~ *gets your heart pumping.* It's a lot like surfing,

except ~~it's done on snow instead of water~~ *snowboarders ride hills, not waves.* I don't know—

there is just something ~~amazing~~ *exhilarating* about zigzagging down a

steep hill at 40 miles per hour. What a rush! The feeling

when the board suddenly leaps into the air is ~~amazing~~ *terrifying*

~~incredible~~ and completely freeing *like launching yourself into space.*

It's ~~really neat~~ *electrifying* to watch expert snowboarders at work,

taking ~~amazing~~ *daredevil* chances. They are just ~~awesome~~ *as confident as a kid going down a slide at the park.*

After a day on the slopes, it feels ~~nice and~~ relaxing to

just kick back and think about all the close calls. ~~It's great~~

~~to know~~ *Knowing* you did something challenging and came through

ready for another run makes you feel unstoppable. it ~~OK~~

©2009. Allyn & Bacon, a division of Pearson Education. Developed by Vicki Spandel. All rights reserved.

Sample D: Revising with Partners

Did you know that some people eat raw oysters?

To people who have never tried it, that might sound

unpleasant   **disgusting.**
~~yucky~~ Or downright ~~gross.~~ For them, it just isn't something

civilized
~~nice~~ people do.

On the other hand, some people think oysters—raw

          a "beachy" treat!   **tastier**
or not—are ~~great!~~ They think they're even ~~better~~ with a

          tangy
spicy sauce or ~~yummy~~ slice of lemon.

                    a bit like grayish pudding or a faceless snail.
          It's true, oysters look ~~a little weird.~~ They look ~~greasy,~~

          a little lumpy.   **slick as a frog leg**
~~oily~~ slippery, and ~~slick.~~ Oysters can feel ~~a little nasty~~ on

                    feels like turning your throat into a water slide.
your tongue. Swallowing them ~~can be an unusual~~

~~experience.~~ But people who eat them often say that the

unexpected
~~special~~ thing about oysters is that with every bite, you get

          delightful—if salt and fish make your mouth water!
the flavor of the sea itself. How ~~amazing is that?~~ Raw or

                    memorable
roasted, oysters definitely make for a ~~special~~ meal!

©2009. Allyn & Bacon, a division of Pearson Education. Developed by Vicki Spandel. All rights reserved.

Freedom of Speech

Trait Connection: **Conventions**

Introduction (Share with students in your own words.)

As we saw in the last lesson, quotation marks set off a speaker's exact words. What falls *inside the quotation marks* is what the speaker said.

We also talked about putting commas and periods inside the quotation marks—when they go with what the person said—like this:

"Cheer up," said Alice.

But George replied, "Not just now."

In this lesson, we're going to give our speakers freedom to say things emphatically or to raise questions. In other words, we're going to bring in **exclamation points** and **question marks**.

Exclamation points and question marks that go with what the speaker says fall inside the quotation marks, just like periods:

"Get out of my room!" yelled Wild Bill.

"Are you speaking to me?" asked the sheriff.

Sometimes, especially when quotation marks are used to set off a title or a short quoted expression, it's the sentence itself that ends with an exclamation point or question mark—and in that case, they fall *outside* the quotation marks. That's because it isn't the expression or title being quoted that is shouting or raising a question, but the sentence itself:

As he said himself, he's a "major procrastinator"!

Did Frank really call himself a "major procrastinator"?

In the practice that follows, Alice and George will have a conversation. In addition, there will be a bit of narration—a continuation of their story in which neither of them speaks. Your job is to put in *all* quotation marks, along with commas, periods, exclamation points, and question marks. Before you begin, read the entire piece through to get the meaning—then read it again, slowly, aloud. To insert commas, use a caret. To insert quotation marks, use an inverted caret. Simply write in periods, exclamation points, and quotation marks.

Teaching the Lesson (General Guidelines for Teachers)

1. Share the examples above, or make up your own examples to practice punctuating dialogue by inserting commas, periods, exclamation points, question marks, and quotation marks in the appropriate places.

2. Encourage students to keep examples handy and refer to them often as they work through this lesson.

3. Share the editing lesson on the following page. Students should read the passage silently and aloud, looking and listening for actual speech, and thinking how best to punctuate it to make it clear.

4. Ask them to edit individually first, then check with a partner. Partners should practice reading aloud (softly) to each other. They do not need to make any changes other than adding punctuation.

5. When everyone is done, ask them to coach you as you edit the same copy.

6. When you finish, read your edited copy aloud, taking time to point out which portions are actual speech, and to indicate why commas, periods, exclamation points (always the editor's choice), or question marks are appropriate in various spots. Compare your edited copy with our suggested text on page 172.

Editing Goal: Punctuate dialogue and other text correctly.
Follow-Up: Review dialogue in your own writing to make sure it is punctuated correctly. Also make sure you have used quotation marks to set off any borrowed material, and that you have cited your source correctly.

©2009. Allyn & Bacon, a division of Pearson Education. Developed by Vicki Spandel. All rights reserved.

Editing Practice

Punctuate dialogue using
- **Quotation marks**
- **Commas**
- **Periods**
- **Exclamation points (optional, but allowed if you think they fit)**
- **Question marks**

Alice was clearly angry I don't want to go she said

I can't see why not said George It will be fabulous

No it won't Alice screamed You know I can't swim

Don't you swim at all George asked

Not one single solitary stroke she replied

You could just float then George suggested hopefully

What if I drown Alice wailed, sounding desperate

George thought about that for a moment, and then

he had an idea I've got it he cried You can use my old

water wings

I'll look ridiculous Alice shrieked

Unfortunately, George was already headed for the

attic to dig up the water wings He kept thinking about Alice

Had she really meant it when she said she did not swim one

single solitary stroke He hoped not

©2009. Allyn & Bacon, a division of Pearson Education. Developed by Vicki Spandel. All rights reserved.

Edited Copy

Text punctuated, using periods, commas, exclamation points, question marks, and quotation marks

Alice was clearly angry. "I don't want to go!" she said.
"I can't see why not," said George. "It will be fabulous!"
"No it won't!" Alice screamed. "You know I can't swim."
"Don't you swim at all?" George asked.
"Not one single solitary stroke," she replied.
"You could just float then," George suggested hopefully.
"What if I drown?" Alice wailed, sounding desperate.

George thought about that for a moment, and then he

had an idea. "I've got it!" he cried. "You can use my old

water wings."

"I'll look ridiculous!" Alice shrieked.

Unfortunately, George was already headed for the

attic to dig up the water wings. He kept thinking about

Alice. Had she really meant it when she said she did not

swim "one single solitary stroke"? He hoped not.

©2009. Allyn & Bacon, a division of Pearson Education. Developed by Vicki Spandel. All rights reserved.

Revising by Trimming

Trait Connection: **Word Choice**

Introduction

Have you noticed that some people come right to the point, while it seems to take others hours to say what's on their minds? In business, technical, and informational writing, high value is placed on getting to the point quickly, and saying *a lot* in a few words. Concise writing gives readers access to more information per word—a sort of linguistic economy, if you will. Writing concisely is a challenge. It requires focusing on what is most meaningful in the message, not padding the writing with unnecessary words and phrases or expressions . . . going on and on, sort of like this, though not *precisely* like this, but you get the idea, somewhat, more or less . . . Enough of *that*. Here's one way to test just how concise a passage is: from each line or two, you should be able to extract enough information to make one statement about something you have learned. If you cannot do that, the writing probably needs trimming. In this lesson, trimming is job number one.

Teacher's Sidebar . . .

Is it possible to cut too much? Yes, actually. Writing can take on a sort of robotic tone—a telegram on the economy plan— if the writer trims *so* much that the very life is squeezed out of the text. We want student writers to keep voice intact, but not make busy readers impatient. Balance is the key.

Focus and Intent

This lesson is intended to help students:

- Appreciate the importance of concise writing.
- Distinguish between wordy and concise writing.
- Revise a wordy piece by trimming *just enough.*

Teaching the Lesson

Step 1: Experimenting with Length

Following are two passages that could use trimming. We've done the first one for you as an example (along with a sample that is potentially over-trimmed). Revise the second by simply crossing out words that are not needed. Feel free to reword anything so that the passage reads smoothly. Make the passage as *short as possible* without trimming so much that the result sounds like robot-speak.

Sample 1

Wordy?

Looking ahead, we all know that communication technologies of the future will bring opportunities for new benefits, but the question remains in our minds about whether those new and wonderful opportunities will make up for the potential loss of privacy we may experience with those new technologies. (47 words)

Trimmed

~~Looking ahead, we all know that~~ Communication technologies of the future will bring ~~opportunities for~~ new benefits, but the question remains ~~in our minds about~~ whether those ~~new and wonderful~~ opportunities will make up for the potential loss of privacy. ~~we may experience with those new technologies.~~ *(25 words)*

Over-Trimmed?

Will technological benefits offset loss of privacy? (7 words)

Sample 2

Wordy?

In case you might be wondering how a ball, such as a soccer ball, gets its bounce, it happens when the ball is kicked, and the kick from someone's foot causes an indentation in the side of the ball, which makes the air inside the ball act like a kind of spring. The ball and the air inside it absorb some of the energy from the kick, and when that energy is later released, it causes the ball to bounce, and it's as simple as that. (86 words)

Trimmed

_____

_____

Over-Trimmed?

_____

Step 2: Making the Reading-Writing Connection

In *Cool Stuff and How It Works*, the authors explain a future technology called "affective computing," a computer's capability to "read" human emotions. Notice how much information these writers pack into a few words:

This technology will enable computers to start gauging our moods and responding to them. Our cars will be able to detect when we are stressed or angry and slow down automatically to reduce the risk of accidents. Our chairs will know when we are bored or tired or frustrated and change their posture to make us feel more relaxed or alert.

(From Chris Woodford, and Luke Collins, Clint Witchalls, Ben Morgan, and James Flint. *Cool Stuff and How It Works.* 2005. New York: DK Publishing. Page 44.)

If you were to make a list of each individual bit of information you gain from this passage, how long do you think that list would be? Try it . . . Now, notice that the passage runs *less than five lines*. That's a lot of information to gain from a relatively short text. What we learn: (1) Affective technology will allow computers to gauge our moods, (2) it will also allow them to respond, (3) cars will detect when we feel stressed or angry, (4) they will slow down as a result, (5) that response will reduce accident risk, (6) chairs will sense our moods, (7) they will shift posture, and (8) that shift will help us feel better.

Step 3: Involving Students as Evaluators

Ask students to review Samples A and B, looking and listening for concise versus wordy writing. Have students work with a partner, noticing which writer practices linguistic economy and which produces text that needs trimming. Encourage students to highlight words or passages they feel could be deleted.

Discussing Results

Most students should identify Sample B as more concise. Sample A needs significant trimming. One trimmed version of Sample A is provided.

Step 4: Modeling Revision

- Share Sample C (*Whole Class Revision*) with students. Read it aloud, listening carefully for wordy passages.

- Talk about whether the writer of Sample C has been economical with words. (Most students should say *no*.) Invite students to coach you through a class revision, carefully identifying words or phrases that could be cut. Feel free to also do some rewriting if you wish. Take care not to over-trim, but make the passage as brief as possible without sacrificing voice or meaning.

- When you finish, read through the entire piece, asking whether your trimming is too light, too heavy, or about right. If you wish, compare your revision with ours, remembering that yours need not match ours in any way.

Step 5: Revising with Partners

Share copies of Sample D (*Revising with Partners*). Ask students to follow the basic steps you modeled with Sample C. *Working with partners,* they should:

- Read the piece aloud, asking themselves whether it is wordy or concise.

- Highlight words or phrases that could be cut.

- Revise by reading aloud, then making final decisions about what should be trimmed and crossing out those words or phrases.

- Read the result aloud to hear the new concise version.

Step 6: Sharing and Discussing Results

When students have finished, ask several pairs of students to share their revisions aloud. Did teams trim the same passages? Did some teams trim more than others? Who was able to achieve the shortest result without sacrificing voice or meaning? (Feel free to share our suggested revision, keeping in mind that students' revisions need not match ours in any way.)

Next Steps

- Ask students to review their own work for wordiness, trimming anything that is not essential to meaning. When they have finished, ask them to put the result to the test by choosing five lines of text at random, and listing all the individual bits of information shared.

- When students share informational writing in response groups, invite listeners to identify *at least three* important bits of information they have gained from the piece, and hand all cards in to the writer. If no one has trouble coming up with three, writers can feel fairly confident that their writing is "information-packed."

- Listen for concise writing in the literature you share with students. Occasionally give them a short passage to analyze. Would they cut anything? How many informational tidbits can they extract from the passage? (Though this lesson focuses on informational writing, this activity also works with personal narrative and fiction.) Recommended:

  - *Cool Stuff and How It Works* by Chris Woodford, and Luke Collins, Clint Witchalls, Ben Morgan, and James Flint. 2005. New York: DK Publishing.

  - *Buzz: The Intimate Bond Between Humans and Insects* by Josie Glausiusz and Volker Steger. 2004. San Francisco: Chronicle Books.

  - *Pocket Babies and Other Amazing Marsupials* by Sneed B. Collard III. 2007. Plain City, OH: Darby Creek Publishing.

  - *Tracking Trash: Flotsam, Jetsam, and the Science of Ocean Motion* by Loree Griffin Burns. 2007. Boston: Houghton Mifflin.

- *For an additional challenge:* Look at letters to the editor or film/book reviews from any newspaper. See if you can cut them by a third. For a super challenge, try cutting them in half. When you can do this without losing meaning, it will noticeably affect the power of your own writing.

Sample A

Concise?
or Wordy?

What we today call the Internet began many years ago in the 1960s when a group of highly clever and innovative people who shared an interest in technology designed a project that would link together the different computers at several universities. Since those long-ago days, the Internet—as we now call it—has grown into a world-wide system that now reaches virtually every country on Earth. It allows us to do many things. We can send emails, music, television programs, informational videos, and many other forms of communication to anyone with Internet access, thus forming a kind of global community. It is even possible for people in the business world to now hold meetings online, so that they no longer have to gather in one place—something that is not always convenient to do. Truly the Internet has changed our whole way of communicating with one another.

(147 words)

©2009. Allyn & Bacon, a division of Pearson Education. Developed by Vicki Spandel. All rights reserved.

Sample B

Concise?
or Wordy?

The antibiotic drug penicillin gets its name from a fungus that is its source: *penicillium*. If you have ever seen moldy bread—bread with a dusty blue coloring—you know what penicillium looks like. The fungus also grows on oranges and cantaloupes. Penicillin was discovered by Scottish scientist Sir Alexander Fleming in 1928, and later developed for use as a medicine.

Penicillin does not kill bacteria outright. Instead, it works by blocking the growth of cell walls. When the walls begin to disintegrate, the bacterium dies.

During World War II, penicillin was widely used to treat soldiers' wounds. It can prevent blood poisoning and gangrene.

Two problems exist with the use of penicillin. One is that some people are allergic to it, and may experience symptoms ranging from rash to fever and diarrhea. The other is that some bacteria have become immune to penicillin and other antibiotics. Scientists are scrambling to find ways of dealing with these so-called "superbugs."

©2009. Allyn & Bacon, a division of Pearson Education. Developed by Vicki Spandel. All rights reserved.

Suggested Revision of Sample A

~~What we today call~~ The Internet began ~~many years ago~~ in the

1960s when a group of ~~highly clever and~~ innovative people, ~~who~~

~~shared an interest in technology~~ designed a ~~project that would~~

way to
link ~~together the different~~ computers at several universities.

then,
Since ~~those long-ago days,~~ the Internet ~~— as we now call it —~~ has

grown into a world-wide system that now reaches virtually

every country on Earth. It allows us to ~~do many things. We can~~

send emails, music, television programs, informational videos,

and many other forms of communication to anyone with

Internet access ~~, thus forming a kind of global community.~~ It is

even possible for people in the business world to ~~now~~ hold

meetings online ~~, so that they no longer have to gather in one~~

~~place — something that is not always convenient to do.~~ Truly the

turned our world into a global community.
Internet has ~~changed our whole way of communicating with~~

~~one another.~~

(From 147 to 86 words)

©2009. Allyn & Bacon, a division of Pearson Education. Developed by Vicki Spandel. All rights reserved.

Sample C: Whole Class Revision

Concise? or Wordy?

The kangaroo, an interesting creature, is a marsupial, meaning it has a pouch for its young. A baby kangaroo, only an inch long at birth, makes its way to the mother's pouch, where it lives for some time, as long as six months to a year.

The smallest kangaroo species is really little, about the size of a rat. The largest, the red kangaroo, may be six feet tall or so and weigh about two hundred pounds. Larger species of kangaroos like to graze together, eating grasses and shrubs, and often graze in small groups called "mobs."

When grazing, kangaroos have a slow "five-legged" gait, moving slowly, and resting on their tails for balance. When they need to move fast, however, they can do it with no problem. In fact, kangaroos can leap as much as 30 feet or more with one bound. They are gentle, but can defend themselves against predators with powerful kicks and claws on their hind feet. They are not defenseless or weak.

(167 words)

©2009. Allyn & Bacon, a division of Pearson Education. Developed by Vicki Spandel. All rights reserved.

Sample D: Revising with Partners

Concise?
or Wordy?

Anyone planning to spend any time at the beach might want to think about getting a tide chart. It is different for every beach, so it is critical to keep that in mind when trying to find the right tide chart. They are available at resorts and marine shops, or you can just get one from the local paper. They almost always have a tide chart if there's a beach nearby.

As soon as one looks at a tide chart, it becomes obvious that high tide comes in later each day because a day is only 24 hours long, and it takes longer than that for the moon to rotate around the earth. So high tide comes later each day. The moon controls the tides, as most people know!

It is helpful to know when high tide and low tide come because it helps to plan activities. For example, high tide is often a good time to go fishing because the tide brings fish closer to shore with it. At least that is the theory! Low tide is a good time for beach combing because when the tide goes out, the beach is uncovered, and it is easier to find treasures.

(201 words)

©2009. Allyn & Bacon, a division of Pearson Education. Developed by Vicki Spandel. All rights reserved.

Suggested Revisions of C and D

Sample C: Whole Class Revision

The kangaroo, ~~an interesting creature~~ is a marsupial, meaning it

has a pouch for its young. A baby kangaroo, only an inch long at birth,

lives in
~~makes its way to~~ the mother's pouch, ~~where it lives for some time, as~~

for
~~long as~~ six months to a year.

The smallest kangaroo species is ~~really little,~~ about the size of a

rat. The largest, the red kangaroo, may be six feet tall ~~or so~~ and weigh

about two hundred pounds. Larger species of kangaroos ~~like to graze~~

~~together, eating grasses and shrubs, and~~ often graze in small groups

called "mobs."

When grazing, kangaroos have a slow "five-legged" gait, ~~moving~~

~~slowly, and~~ resting on their tails for balance. When they need to move

fast, however, they can ~~do it with no problem. In fact, kangaroos can~~

leap as much as 30 feet or more with one bound. They are gentle, but

can defend themselves against predators with powerful kicks and claws

on their hind feet. ~~They are not defenseless or weak~~

(From 167 to 124 words)

©2009. Allyn & Bacon, a division of Pearson Education. Developed by Vicki Spandel. All rights reserved.

Sample D: Revising with Partners

Anyone planning to spend any time at the beach might want to think about

getting a tide chart. ~~It~~ —something that is different for every beach, ~~so it is critical to keep~~

~~that in mind when trying to find the right tide chart. They~~ Tide charts are available at

resorts and marine shops, or ~~you can just get one~~ from ~~the~~ any local paper, with

~~They almost always have a tide chart if there's~~ a beach nearby.

~~As soon as one looks at a tide chart, it becomes obvious that high~~

~~tide comes in later each day.~~ Because a day is only 24 hours long, and it

takes longer than that for the moon to rotate around the earth, ~~So~~ high tide

comes later each day. The moon controls the tides. ~~as most people know!~~

Knowing times for

~~It is helpful to know when~~ high tide and low tide ~~come because it~~ makes it easier

~~helps~~ to plan activities. For example, high tide is often a good time to go

fishing because the tide brings fish closer to shore. ~~with it. At least that~~

~~is the theory!~~ At low tide, ~~is a good time for beach combing because when~~

beachcombing treasures are easier to spot!

~~the tide goes out, the beach is uncovered, and it is easier to find treasures.~~

(From 201 to 119 words)

©2009. Allyn & Bacon, a division of Pearson Education. Developed by Vicki Spandel. All rights reserved.

New Person, New Paragraph

Trait Connection: **Conventions**

Introduction (Share with students in your own words.)

There's one more important piece to the quotation mark puzzle (more than one, actually, but one more *we're* going to tackle). It's about paragraphing. Up until now, we've been doing all the paragraphing for you. Did you notice? How'd we do? Let's hope you were paying attention because this time around, paragraphing is up to you. No worries. It's simple. When a new person speaks, you begin a new paragraph—like this:

> "Did you feed my turtle?" asked Mildred. She could see that the poor little critter still looked hungry, and Amos had a very guilty look on his face.
>
> "I thought," Amos replied, "that was *my* hamburger!"

Paragraphing is extremely handy *for the reader* if you are writing dialogue and choose not to identify the speaker each time. It does get a little dreary to be continually saying, *he said, she said, he said, she said*. Paragraphing helps sort things out, so you do not need to label *every* speech. Let's see if you can tell where the paragraphs should go in the following sample—and by the way, you can mark a paragraph with a mark that looks like a capital letter P, only backward, and with double lines, like this: ¶ Notice we indented the first paragraph for you.

> It was growing chilly. Kate hugged her flimsy jacket around her shoulders. "Let's head home, Dina," she said, shivering. "I don't want to," Dina answered. "The game isn't finished, and I don't want to miss the end." "Who cares if we miss the end?" "I do! I've watched this much. Come on—I'll lend you my jacket, you wimp!"

Did you find that easy? How many paragraphs were there in all? If you said two—well, that's not quite enough. Three? Getting there—but you might have missed one change of speaker. If you said four, spot on. You paid close attention to who was speaking. Your marked up text should look like this:

184

It was growing chilly. Kate hugged her flimsy jacket around her shoulders. "Let's head home, Dina," she said, shivering. ¶"I don't want to," Dina answered. "The game isn't finished, and I don't want to miss the end." ¶"Who cares if we miss the end?" ¶"I do! I've watched this much. Come on—I'll lend you my jacket, you wimp!"

In the practice that follows, you'll need to insert all the paragraphs. As in the last lesson, the text is a mix of speech and narration. You must read it closely to determine when people are talking. There are two speakers—Ellen and her brother, Ticker. Just to make things interesting, we have omitted a few essential punctuation marks, so read carefully, silently and aloud. Look for missing quotation marks (sometimes the first set is there, but not the second), and missing commas, periods, or question marks.

Teaching the Lesson (General Guidelines for Teachers)

1. Share the examples above, or make up your own examples to practice determining where to start a new paragraph with two speakers plus narration.

2. Encourage students to keep these examples handy and refer to them often as they work through this lesson.

3. As necessary for your students, review editorial marks and their use: carets, inverted carets, and the paragraph symbol.

4. Share the editing lesson on the following page. Students should read the passage silently and aloud, looking and listening for speech, and thinking how to punctuate it to make it clear.

5. Ask them to edit individually first, then check with a partner.

6. When everyone is done, ask them to coach you as you edit the same copy.

7. When you finish, read your edited copy aloud, taking time to point out which portions are actual speech, and to indicate why certain punctuation or a new paragraph is needed. Compare your edited copy with our suggested text on page 187. We have marked paragraphs, but also indented them so they are easier to visualize.

**Editing Goal: Insert 10 missing marks of punctuation. Mark 12 paragraphs.
Follow-Up: Review dialogue in your own writing to make sure it
is punctuated correctly and paragraphs begin where they should.
Also make sure you have used quotation marks to set off any
borrowed material, and that you have cited your source correctly.**

Editing Practice

Mark new paragraphs
Punctuate dialogue using
- **Quotation marks**
- **Commas**
- **Periods**
- **Exclamation points (optional, but OK if *you* think they fit)**
- **Question marks**

"Tell me a ghost story " said Ticker. "I don't believe in ghosts " said Ellen. She was brushing her hair, getting ready to go to the movies with her friend, B. J. "I don't either, Ticker said. " But I believe in ghost stories—and you have to tell me one before you go." "What?? Says who " "Says me. Your dumb old hair looks good enough. So, can you tell me one really short story? "I don't have time, Ticker." "Do so!" "Tell you what. I'll tell you a story when I get back, all right? Ellen grabbed her purse, slipped her hairbrush into it, and was out the door. "Have fun " Ticker called. He pressed his face against the screen door. "Hey—do you want to go " "Really? Ticker couldn't believe his sister was asking him anywhere. "Is the movie about ghosts?" No—but come anyway. Hurry up, though, or we'll be late." They took off together, at a run.

©2009. Allyn & Bacon, a division of Pearson Education. Developed by Vicki Spandel. All rights reserved.

Edited Copy

Text punctuated
Paragraphs marked

¶ "Tell me a ghost story," said Ticker.

¶ "I don't believe in ghosts," said Ellen. She was brushing her hair, getting ready to go to the movies with her friend, B. J.

¶ "I don't either," Ticker said. "But I believe in ghost stories—and you have to tell me one before you go."

¶ "What?? Says who?"

¶ "Says me. Your dumb old hair looks good enough. So, can you tell me one really short story?"

¶ "I don't have time, Ticker."

¶ "Do so!"

¶ "Tell you what. I'll tell you a story when I get back, all right?" Ellen grabbed her purse, slipped her hairbrush into it, and was out the door.

¶ "Have fun," Ticker called. He pressed his face against the screen door.

¶ "Hey—do you want to go?"

¶ "Really?" Ticker couldn't believe his sister was asking him anywhere. "Is the movie about ghosts?"

¶ "No—but come anyway. Hurry up, though, or we'll be late." They took off together, at a run.

©2009. Allyn & Bacon, a division of Pearson Education. Developed by Vicki Spandel. All rights reserved.

Revising with the Just Right Word

Lesson 23

Trait Connection: **Word Choice**

Introduction

At some time or other, you've probably found yourself unable to call up *just* the right word *just* when you needed it. You're trying to tell a friend about someone with a rude personality—but *rude* isn't quite it. *Brusque?* Too breezy. *Blunt?* Too forceful. *Gruff, surly, sullen, touchy, moody?* No, no, no, no—and no. *Thorny?* Yes—*that's* it! *Thorny*—like running headlong into a prickly tree. As warm and fuzzy as a cactus. A porcupine sort of personality. In some situations, *thorny* says things that *rude*—or another close cousin—doesn't quite capture. The *just right* word makes all the difference. Of course, as a writer, only you can know what is just right. This makes revising someone else's text a bit tricky (*puzzling, knotty, perplexing, challenging*). You must first decide in your own mind what the writer is trying to say—get a picture if you can—then choose the words that make the message clear and memorable.

Teacher's Sidebar . . .
In this lesson, students are given alternative words with which to work in doing their revision. They are not bound by these choices at all. They should feel free to use a thesaurus or book of synonyms to identify other possibilities—or even to rework sentences to say things another way. Think of the sidebar synonyms as a place *to begin*.

Focus and Intent

This lesson is intended to help students:

- Appreciate the importance of the "just right" word.
- Recognize how subtle shades of meaning affect the message.
- Revise a piece by choosing words that are "just right" for the moment—message, audience, and mood.

Teaching the Lesson

Step 1: Shading the Meaning

Following are several passages in which one critical word has yet to be selected. Several alternatives are offered. No particular alternative is "right." The point of the activity is to discuss how even slight changes in wording influence meaning or imagery or mood. Feel free to consult a dictionary or thesaurus as you go through the examples—and feel free to come up with another word or phrase entirely if you and your students think of a better way to say it.

Sample 1

*Games, books, papers, clothes, and bits of half-eaten meals decorated every inch of floor space, every surface of furniture, and both windowsills. A picture of Mick's room should really be in the dictionary, right next to the word (**messy, grungy, piggy, cluttered, topsy-turvy**).*

Sample 2

*Izzy had studied for hours for the geography test. But when she opened the test booklet, not a single map looked familiar. She couldn't identify one river or mountain range. Had she been studying out of the wrong textbook?! Izzy felt felt her pulse racing. She was totally (**puzzled, confused, mystified, stumped, flustered**).*

Sample 3

*It was one of those rare and beautiful spring sunrises. Brilliant and golden, the sun rose into a cloudless sky. The meadow, still damp with the morning dew, (**glared, shimmered, gleamed, sparkled, blazed**) under its first rays.*

Sample 4

*Roy's right boot was squeezing his foot hard—he should have gotten a bigger size. His sock was worn clear through, and now the rough leather was (**scraping, eroding, scratching, chafing, bothering**) his skin.*

Step 2: Making the Reading-Writing Connection

In *The Schwa Was Here*, narrator Antsy tells us that "going to the movies with Lexie was like taking an Honors English class." Lexie is visually impaired, and though she can hear the movie just fine, she depends on Antsy to let her know what's happening onscreen. What's more, Lexie demands a precise interpretation, as in this scene where a character in the film is attempting to elude an alien monster (Lexie speaks first):

"How is she walking?"
"I don't know—like a person walks."
"Is she strolling, meandering, stalking?"
"Storming," I said. "She's storming down the hallway toward the air lock."

(From Neal Shusterman. *The Schwa Was Here*. 2004. New York: Puffin. Page 127.)

Do you like Antsy's word choice in this passage? Without having the advantage of seeing the movie firsthand, do you think any of Lexie's suggestions—*strolling, meandering,* or *stalking*— would have worked as well as *storming* to describe a woman trying to escape from a movie monster? Can you think of another word (other than *storming*) that might capture the frenzy of this moment?

Step 3: Involving Students as Evaluators

Ask students to review Samples A and B, particularly noticing the underlined words. Have students work with a partner, thinking about whether each underlined word is a good choice or whether they might use an alternative. Encourage students to write their own alternative word choices in the margin.

Discussing Results

Most students should identify Sample B as stronger. The writer of Sample A seems to have settled for the first word that came to mind. One possible revision of Sample A is provided, along with additional alternatives in the margin. Students should feel free to opt for a different choice from ours.

Step 4: Modeling Revision

- Share Sample C (*Whole Class Revision*) with students. Read it aloud, looking carefully at the four underlined words and the alternatives included in the margin.

- Talk about whether the writer of Sample C has made the best word choice, given the message and mood of the piece. (Most students should say *no.*) Invite students to coach you through a class revision, discussing alternatives, and together choosing the best word for the context. Feel free to insert your own original choices if you think of a stronger word or phrase than any of those suggested.

- When you finish, read through the entire piece, asking whether your choices make the message clear and memorable. If you wish, compare your revision with ours, remembering that your word choice need not match ours.

Step 5: Revising with Partners

Share copies of Sample D (*Revising with Partners*). Ask students to follow the basic steps you modeled with Sample C. *Working with partners,* they should:

- Read the piece aloud, asking themselves whether the underlined words are a good fit—or not.

- Discuss alternatives for each of the underlined words.

- Use a dictionary, thesaurus, book of synonyms, or any other available resource in making final choices.

- Read the result aloud to hear the difference a more thoughtful word choice makes.

Step 6: Sharing and Discussing Results

When students have finished, ask several pairs of students to share their revisions aloud. Did teams make the same word choices? Did any teams come up with their own alternatives? (Feel free to share our suggested revision, keeping in mind that students' revisions need not match ours in any way.)

Next Steps

- Ask students to review their own writing for word choice, underlining one or two words they would like to change—or consider changing. Encourage them to use a thesaurus or other resource to explore possibilities. It is startling how much difference changing even *one word* makes.

- When students meet in response groups, invite them to give listeners a list of options for two or three words—just as in the examples from this lesson. When listeners have agreed on their choice, the writer can compare it with what he or she chose, and discuss which works better.

- Choose any passage from literature that is particularly strong in word choice. Share it with students, but replace two, three, or more of the words with flatter, more mundane alternatives. Underline or boldface those words to make them stand out. Then invite students to brainstorm better choices. When they have made their choices, compare them with the author's original selection. Do they prefer the author's originals—or their own choices?

- Listen for strong word choice in the literature you share with students. Keep a class list of favorite words, or invite students to enter them into a personal writing journal. Recommended:
  - *The Schwa Was Here* by Neal Shusterman. 2004. New York: Puffin.
  - *Exiled: Memoirs of a Camel* by Kathleen Karr. 2006. Tarrytown, NY: Marshall Cavendish.
  - *Miss Spitfire: Reaching Helen Keller* by Sarah Miller. 2007. Boston: Atheneum.
  - *Nature by Design* by Bruce Brooks. 1991. New York: Farrar, Straus, and Giroux.
  - *The Wednesday Wars* by Gary D. Schmidt. 2007. New York: Clarion.

- *For an additional challenge:* Invite students to choose a passage from any published work—newspaper, periodical, or book. Ask them to revise it by changing three or more words or phrases to something stronger—then present both versions to the class. Can their classmates identify the original and the revision? Which is stronger?

Sample A

Just right?

Dirk was busily <u>going</u> through his closet, using only his left

hand, desperately trying to come up with something to

wear for his grandmother's ninetieth birthday. He had badly

<u>hurt</u> his right index finger on a paint can, and had bandaged

it with an old sock—not such a good idea, probably, but it

would do until he could come up with a better idea.

As he reached for his red shirt, Dirk recalled that he

had not yet gotten his grandmother a gift. She wasn't the

sort to just like flowers, like other grandmothers. She was

extremely <u>strong</u> for ninety, and had rather <u>strange</u> hobbies

for a senior citizen of her years, including biking and

kayaking. "Maybe I should get her a new paddle for her

kayak," he thought, and the idea made him laugh. He could

picture the clerk saying, "Are you *sure* this is for your

grandmother?"

rummaging, digging, foraging, poking, shuffling, going

bruised, bumped, injured, scratched, damaged, scraped, hurt

rowdy, strong, sturdy, robust, tough, feisty

unusual, different, surprising, remarkable, strange

©2009. Allyn & Bacon, a division of Pearson Education. Developed by Vicki Spandel. All rights reserved.

Sample B

Just right?

Almost without breathing, Alec reached into his tackle box,

his fingers feeling for the fly he had tied just last night. A

big salmon was <u>hovering</u> right in the shadow of a large

hovering, waiting, lingering, floating, oscillating

rock, no more than six feet from shore. Alec meant to <u>snag</u>

him. This would be his first catch in a long time. It would

snatch, catch, hook, snag, capture

surprise his dad, who had been fly fishing for years, and

had yet to catch anything <u>rivaling</u> this big fellow. It was

matching, challenging, rivaling, competing with, exceeding, outdoing

catch and release, so he would have to let him go—but Alec

didn't mind. He admired the strength and courage of the

salmon. Plus, he meant to get a picture before he released

the fish, so he could show this prize to his dad. With the fly

now secure on his line, Alec rose silently, and cast out just

past the fish. He reeled in slowly, slowly, waiting for the

go for, grab, snatch, bite, chomp, take

fish to <u>take</u> the fly.

©2009. Allyn & Bacon, a division of Pearson Education. Developed by Vicki Spandel. All rights reserved.

193

Suggested Revision of Sample A

Dirk was busily ~~going~~ rummaging through his closet, using only his left

hand, desperately trying to come up with something to

wear for his grandmother's ninetieth birthday. He had badly

~~hurt~~ scraped his right index finger on a paint can, and had bandaged

it with an old sock—not such a good idea, probably, but it

would do until he could come up with a better idea.

rummaging, digging, foraging, poking, shuffling, going

bruised, bumped, injured, scratched, damaged, scraped, hurt

　　As he reached for his red shirt, Dirk recalled that he

had not yet gotten his grandmother a gift. She wasn't the

sort to just like flowers, like other grandmothers. She was

extremely ~~strong~~ feisty for ninety, and had rather ~~strange~~ remarkable hobbies

for a senior citizen of her years, including biking and

kayaking. "Maybe I should get her a new paddle for her

kayak," he thought, and the idea made him laugh. He could

picture the clerk saying, "Are you *sure* this is for your

grandmother?"

rowdy, strong, sturdy, robust, tough, feisty

unusual, different, surprising, remarkable, strange

©2009. Allyn & Bacon, a division of Pearson Education. Developed by Vicki Spandel. All rights reserved.

Sample C: Whole Class Revision

Just right?

The canoe <u>floated</u> briskly over the water, riding the waves toward the shore. The two boys, Toby and Chance, <u>stepped</u> out as the bow raked over the sand and mud at the water's edge. Chance tossed the thick rope to Toby, who tied the canoe snugly to a sturdy birch tree. They looked around.

The island seemed deserted. Out of nowhere, a <u>bad</u> mountain of fur scrambled down the rocks and headed right for them, growling and baring its teeth. Only then did Chance remember how well bears can swim. Scrambling to undo the knot around the birch, Toby found himself panting for breath. Chance had already leaped into the canoe and was back-paddling by the time Toby <u>hurried</u> through the water and leaped aboard.

floated, glided, sailed, slipped, drifted

jumped, hopped, bounded, vaulted, leaped, stepped

ferocious, fierce, deadly, vicious, bad, demonic, nasty

hustled, hastened, rushed, scurried, splashed, tore, ripped, hurried

©2009. Allyn & Bacon, a division of Pearson Education. Developed by Vicki Spandel. All rights reserved.

Sample D: Revising with Partners

Just right?

Betsy had only wanted an after-school job—just to make a little money. She'd had no idea what a <u>hard thing</u> it would be, watching two small children. Kevin, the younger child, was constantly <u>crying</u>. The older child, Olivia, was a <u>difficult person</u>. She was forever teasing Kevin, taking his toys, hiding things, or spilling her food deliberately. Betsy told herself to hang in there because she really needed the money. On one particularly bad day, though, Betsy didn't know if she could take much more pressure. She <u>walked</u> into the bathroom, slammed the door, and yelled as loudly as she could to no one in particular. *There.* That felt better. Calmer now, she returned to the battle of Kevin and Olivia.

hardship, challenge, problem, difficulty, crisis

screaming, screeching, making a racket, carrying on

nightmare, pain in the neck, pest, nuisance

stormed, marched, lurched, sauntered, strolled, stomped, shuffled, strode

©2009. Allyn & Bacon, a division of Pearson Education. Developed by Vicki Spandel. All rights reserved.

Suggested Revisions of C and D

Sample C: Whole Class Revision

The canoe ~~floated~~ glided briskly over the water, riding the waves

floated, glided, sailed, slipped, drifted

toward the shore. The two boys, Toby and Chance, ~~stepped~~ hopped

out as the bow raked over the sand and mud at the water's

edge. Chance tossed the thick rope to Toby, who tied the

jumped, hopped, bounded, vaulted, leaped, stepped

canoe snugly to a sturdy birch tree. They looked around.

The island seemed deserted. Out of nowhere, a ~~bad~~ ferocious

ferocious, fierce, deadly, vicious, bad, demonic, nasty

mountain of fur scrambled down the rocks and headed right

for them, growling and baring its teeth. Only then did

Chance remember how well bears can swim. Scrambling to

undo the knot around the birch, Toby found himself panting

for breath. Chance had already leaped into the canoe and

hustled, hastened, rushed, scurried, splashed, tore, ripped, hurried

was back-paddling by the time Toby ~~hurried~~ ripped through the

water and leaped aboard.

©2009. Allyn & Bacon, a division of Pearson Education. Developed by Vicki Spandel. All rights reserved.

Sample D: Revising with Partners

Betsy had only wanted an after-school job—just to make a

little money. She'd had no idea what a ~~hard thing~~ it would   *challenge*

be, watching two small children. Kevin, the younger child,

was constantly ~~crying~~ The older child, Olivia, was a   *making a racket.*

~~difficult person.~~ She was forever teasing Kevin, taking his   *pest.*

toys, hiding things, or spilling her food deliberately. Betsy

told herself to hang in there because she really needed the

money. On one particularly bad day, though, Betsy didn't

know if she could take much more pressure. She ~~walked~~   *stormed*

into the bathroom, slammed the door, and yelled as loudly

as she could to no one in particular. *There*. That felt better.

Calmer now, she returned to the battle of Kevin and Olivia.

hardship, challenge, problem, difficulty, crisis

screaming, screeching, making a racket, carrying on

nightmare, pain in the neck, pest, nuisance

stormed, marched, lurched, sauntered, strolled, stomped, shuffled, strode

©2009. Allyn & Bacon, a division of Pearson Education. Developed by Vicki Spandel. All rights reserved.

Lie or Lay?

Trait Connection: **Conventions**

Introduction (Share with students in your own words.)

Two words often confused in English are the verbs *lie* (as in *lie down*, not *tell a lie*) and *lay*. It's easier to tell the difference if you remember that *lie* means to <u>recline</u>, while *lay* means to <u>set down</u>:

> I love to *lie* in the hammock and watch the stars.
> *Lay* the book on the table.

Now here's where it gets a little tricky—but practice will help you to use the right form. The past tense of *lie* is *lay*. The past perfect (time *before* recent events) is *lain*. So—

> Sherry wants to *lie* on the couch and watch TV.
> She *lay* there for just ten minutes, and then fell asleep.
> When she *had lain* there for an hour, the phone rang.

The past tense of *lay* is *laid*, and past perfect (time *before* recent events) is also *laid*. So—

> I *laid* my wallet on the table.
> I thought I *laid* my wallet right by this book.
> If I *had laid* my wallet here, I'd be able to find it now.

See if you can fill in the right words for the following sentences. Each one will be a form of *lie* or *lay:*

> The groceries were so heavy, Bill had to _____ them down.
> In fact, he had to ___ down himself!
> He _____ the groceries on the floor, by the door.
> Then, he _____ down on the couch—just for a minute.
> Bill didn't realize he had _____ the grocery bag near the heat register.

> When he had _____ on the couch for a few minutes, he heard a shriek. It was Martha—telling him the ice cream had melted.

> If he had _____ the groceries outside on the icy front step, that might not have happened!

Let's see how you did. Remember, everything Bill does himself is a form of *lie*—meaning to <u>recline</u>. Everything Bill does with the groceries is a form of *lay*—meaning to <u>set down</u>. Here are the correct words for each sentence:

> The groceries were so heavy, Bill had to <u>lay</u> them down.
>
> In fact, he had to <u>lie</u> down himself!
>
> He <u>laid</u> the groceries on the floor, by the door.
>
> Then, he <u>lay</u> down on the couch—just for a minute.
>
> Bill didn't realize he <u>had laid</u> the grocery bag near the heat register.
>
> When he <u>had lain</u> on the couch for a few minutes, he heard a shriek. It was Martha—telling him the ice cream had melted.
>
> If he <u>had laid</u> the groceries outside on the icy front step, that might not have happened!

If you found that warm-up easy, this lesson will be a piece of cake. In order not to confuse you with incorrect words, we have simply left blanks, as in the sentences you just completed. Your job is to fill in the blanks with the correct form of *lie* or *lay*. Please don't *lie* down or *lay* your pencil down until you're done!

Teaching the Lesson (General Guidelines for Teachers)

1. Share the examples above, or make up your own examples to practice using the correct forms of *lie* and *lay*.

2. Encourage students to keep examples handy and refer to them often as they work through this lesson.

3. Share the editing lesson on the following page. Students should read the passage silently, filling in blanks with the correct forms—and rereading aloud to check their work.

4. Ask them to edit individually first, then check with a partner.

5. When everyone is done, ask them to coach you as you edit the same copy.

6. When you finish, read your edited copy aloud, taking time to discuss reasons behind your choices. Compare your edited copy with our suggested text on page 202.

7. If students have any difficulty, revisit the warm-up, make up an additional warm-up of your own, and then repeat the lesson.

**Editing Goal: Use the correct forms of <u>lie</u> and <u>lay</u> to fill in 11 blanks.
Follow-Up: Review your own writing to make sure
you have used forms of <u>lie</u> and <u>lay</u> correctly.**

Editing Practice

Use the correct form of each word:
- **Lie** *(recline): lie, lying, lay, had lain, have lain*
- **Lay** *(set down): lay, laying, laid, had laid, have laid*

Sue _____ down her pencil in disgust. She had been editing the manuscript for hours! She was exhausted—and frustrated. "I need to ____ down," she sighed. She glanced at her watch, which she had taken off and _____ on the desk. It was only 7 o'clock. She checked two more spellings in the dictionary, then _____ it next to her watch. Her cat Murphy was growing restless. He liked to _____ on the desk to be near Sue while she worked. But it was past dinner time for Murph. He had _____ there patiently for almost two hours. Now he needed a good stretch—and some food! "OK, Murph," she said, with a smile. "Five more minutes and I promise to ____ down my pencil and make dinner for both of us. Then we'll both _____ on the couch and watch a movie! Now . . . where did I ____ that eraser . . . ah!" It was _____ right under Murphy, just where Sue had _____ it earlier.

©2009. Allyn & Bacon, a division of Pearson Education. Developed by Vicki Spandel. All rights reserved.

Edited Copy

The correct form of each word used:
- **Lie** *(recline): lie, lying, lay, had lain, have lain*
- **Lay** *(set down): lay, laying, laid, had laid, have laid*

Sue **lay** down her pencil in disgust. She had been editing the manuscript for hours! She was exhausted—and frustrated. "I need to **lie** down," she sighed. She glanced at her watch, which she had taken off and **laid** on the desk. It was only 7 o'clock. She checked two more spellings in the dictionary, then **laid** it next to her watch. Her cat Murphy was growing restless. He liked to **lie** on the desk to be near Sue while she worked. But it was past dinner time for Murph. He had **lain** there patiently for almost two hours. Now he needed a good stretch—and some food! "OK, Murph," she said, with a smile. "Five more minutes and I promise to **lay** down my pencil and make dinner for both of us. Then we'll both **lie** on the couch and watch a movie! Now . . . where did I **lay** that eraser . . . ah!" It was **lying** right under Murphy, just where Sue had **laid** it earlier.

©2009. Allyn & Bacon, a division of Pearson Education. Developed by Vicki Spandel. All rights reserved.

Revising to Go Parallel

Trait Connection: **Sentence Fluency**

Introduction

If you have ever watched a group of professional dancers or synchronized swimmers perform, you know how important it is for everyone to make the same moves at the same time. If they don't, it looks as if everyone is doing his or her own version of the performance. When they *do* come together, the result is graceful and rhythmic. In writing, the closest thing to synchronized swimming is called *parallel structure.* In parallel structure, different parts of the sentence follow the same patterns, like this: *She turned, she bowed, and she departed.* Or like this: *He was good with dogs, excellent with cars, and irresponsible with money.* Do you hear the rhythm of the pattern? To see the difference between parallel and non-parallel structure, let's take the synchronicity out of that second sentence: *He was good with dogs, and cars were among his special interests, but when it came to money, no one trusted him.* This sentence says basically the same thing, but in three different patterns. And poof—there goes the rhythm. The mind *loves* patterns. When you frame your message in a pattern, you draw attention to it—just as dancers moving in harmony draw your eye.

Teacher's Sidebar . . .

It is perfectly possible to write grammatical sentences without using parallel structure. But it adds force to writing, particularly when the most important element of the sentence is saved for last. Readers love that build-up to the punchline. Notice that parallel structure works with single words, phrases, clauses, or whole sentences. It is most striking when not overdone. One or two samples per passage yield just the right punch.

Focus and Intent

This lesson is intended to help students:

- Understand what parallel structure is.
- Recognize parallel structure in text.
- Revise a piece by creating parallel structure.

Teaching the Lesson

Step 1: Using Your Ears

Parallel structure is visible on the page because of the repetition of patterns. But often, the best way to recognize it is to listen. Parallels often come in three's, and if you listen carefully, you will also notice that the third element tends to be the most significant. Writers create this pattern on purpose because they know readers love it when the writer leads up to a key point. Look and listen carefully to the following sentences. Mark each parallel structure sentence with a check (✓) in the blank. Then see if you can revise the others to make them parallel in structure. The first two are done for you.

___✓___ 1. Tessa stared at the blank page, seized her pen, and wrote her way into history. [She *stared*, she *seized*, she *wrote*]

_____ 2. Alberta noticed that her hair was a bit messy, the crookedness of her hat bothered her, and somehow caked mud had gotten on her skirt.

   Alberta noticed that her hair was messy, her hat was crooked, and her skirt was caked with mud.

_____ 3. Pirates are sneaky, they don't like to bathe much, and most people are frightened of them.

_____ 4. The dog ran across the porch, leaped over the fence, and sailed into Becky's waiting arms.

_____ 5. August tends to be hot, the rainfall is generally low, and people run out of things to do.

_____ 6. Rain poured down in buckets, wind tore our flimsy sail to ribbons, and relentless waves ripped at the bindings that held our raft together.

Step 2: Making the Reading-Writing Connection

In *Hatchet*, author Gary Paulsen treats us to a serving of parallel construction that actually contains small parallels within the larger parallel. The story's hero, Brian, has just captured a bird he describes as a little, fat "flying pear" (p. 142). It's actually a grouse. Brian is starving, and can hardly bear to wait until the bird is cooked enough that he can pull off the first bite and slip it into his mouth:

> *Never in all the food, all the hamburgers and malts, all the fries or meals at home, never in all the candy or pies or cakes, never in all the roasts or steaks or pizzas, never in all the submarine sandwiches, never never never had he tasted anything as fine as that first bite.*

(From Gary Paulsen. *Hatchet: 20th Anniversary Edition*. 2007. New York: Simon and Schuster. Page 146.)

Can you find all the patterns? How does repetition of all the "never" expressions add momentum and force to this particular passage? Notice the "never never never" at the end. Any usual punctuation missing? Right—no commas. Why do you suppose Paulsen would leave them out just at this moment? Notice the very last thing

Paulsen mentions at the end of the sentence: "that first bite." What is the impact of saving this for last? Imagine if he had written instead, "That first bite was better than any pies, cakes, burgers, or steaks I had ever had." What difference would that order of things make? (If you have the 20th Anniversary Edition of the book, do not miss Paulsen's description of "The Foolbirds," page 140.)

Step 3: Involving Students as Evaluators

Ask students to review Samples A and B, particularly looking and listening for parallel structure. Have students work with a partner, thinking about whether each writer uses parallel structure or misses opportunities to do so. Encourage students to underline parallel patterns and to make marginal notes about creating parallel patterns in other sentences.

Discussing Results

Most students should identify Sample A as the one with parallel structure. The writer of Sample B has opportunities to use parallel structure, but has chosen not to. One possible revision of Sample B, showing the difference parallel structure might make, is provided. You may wish to ask students to practice putting sentences into parallel form prior to sharing our example.

Step 4: Modeling Revision

- Share Sample C (*Whole Class Revision*) with students. Read it aloud, looking and listening for examples of parallel structure.

- Talk about whether the writer of Sample C has used parallel structure anywhere in the piece. (Most students should say *no*.) Invite students to coach you through a class revision, discussing when and where parallel structure might make a difference and revising accordingly. Go for two revisions. Too much parallel structure can be overkill; you want to use it sparingly so that it retains its punch.

- When you finish, read through the entire piece, asking whether your choices give the sentences more power. If you wish, compare your revision with ours, remembering that your particular sentence patterns need not match ours exactly—and that we may have chosen to use more parallel structure for modeling purposes.

Step 5: Revising with Partners

Share copies of Sample D (*Revising with Partners*). Ask students to follow the basic steps you modeled with Sample C. *Working with partners,* they should:

- Read the piece aloud, asking themselves whether the author has opted to use parallel structure—or not.

- Discuss when and where they might use parallel structure to give sentences additional rhythm and power.

- Sketch out a draft or two on scratch paper prior to entering the final choice into the revision text.

■ Read the result aloud to hear the difference parallel structure can make in the drama and power of sentences.

Step 6: Sharing and Discussing Results

When students have finished, ask several pairs of students to share their revisions aloud. Did teams transform the same sentences? Did they use the same patterns? Compare your final draft with ours if you wish, noting that we may have used more parallel structure for modeling purposes.

Next Steps

■ Practice parallel structure using the Gary Paulsen sample (*Making the Reading-Writing Connection*) as a model. Ask students to write a similar sentence, based on any topic they choose: e.g., favorite food, best book, great ski run, exhilarating swimming competition; worst test, unforgettable storm, or personal encounter.

■ Ask students to review their own writing for parallel structure, perhaps modifying one passage (two or three at most) to fit this pattern. Encourage them to draft possibilities on scratch paper until they find the one they like best.

■ In response groups, students can support one another by brainstorming various ways to build parallel structure into one sentence, selected by the writer. More than one revision is possible, and as you find samples you like in literature (such as Paulsen's), save and post them, so that students can use them as models.

■ Listen for parallel structure in the literature you share with students. Save favorites, and post them as models. Recommended:

● *Hatchet* by Gary Paulsen. 2007. New York: Simon and Schuster.

● *Lizzie Bright and the Buckminster Boy* by Gary D. Schmidt. 2006. New York: Yearling.

● *Maniac Magee* by Jerry Spinelli. 2002. New York: Scholastic.

● *The Miraculous Journey of Edward Toulane* by Kate DiCamillo. 2006. Cambridge, MA: Candlewick Press.

● *Peter and the Secret of Rundoon* by Dave Barry and Ridley Pearson. 2007. New York: Hyperion (Disney Editions).

■ *For an additional challenge:* Parallel structure is particularly effective in persuasive pieces because it gives a dramatic sound to the rhetoric. Invite students to investigate famous speeches online to see if they can identify any samples of parallel structure—and if they find one, to perform it orally for the class so everyone can hear the impact. (Suggestions: Winston Churchill, John F. Kennedy, Chief Joseph, Dr. Martin Luther King, Jr.)

Sample A

Parallel
Structure?

Robin was tall for her age, slightly underweight, and highly

athletic. She pondered whether to join the school's track

team, though—unsure whether she had the speed it would

take. Most of her athletic experience focused on team

sports: basketball, which she loved; soccer, which she liked

reasonably well; and softball, which she tolerated only

because it had been her mom's favorite sport in school.

Now, she was considering doing something different,

something that would be just for herself. The lone

competitor. The idea made her smile . . . and hesitate . . .

and bite her nails. What if she wasn't all that good?

©2009. Allyn & Bacon, a division of Pearson Education. Developed by Vicki Spandel. All rights reserved.

Sample B

Parallel
Structure?

The spider looks long and hard for a suitable place to build its web. When it finds a sturdy support, such as a tree trunk or door frame, it throws out a dragline, taking time to attach it securely to the structure. Once the dragline is in place, the spider spins a sturdy frame that will hold the web together. Spokes come next, making the web resemble an old-fashioned wagon wheel, and finally, the spinning of crosslines connects the spokes tightly. These give the web its strength. Spiders are good engineers with built-in skill at designing. They hunt really patiently, too. If no prey arrives immediately, the spider will wait. In addition, the spider has resilience. It can go without food a long time if it has water.

©2009. Allyn & Bacon, a division of Pearson Education. Developed by Vicki Spandel. All rights reserved.

Suggested Revision of Sample B

The spider looks long and hard for a suitable place to build

its web. When it finds a sturdy support, such as a tree trunk

or door frame, it throws out a dragline, taking time to attach

it securely to the structure. Once the dragline is in place,

the spider spins a sturdy frame that ~~will hold~~ **holds** the web

together**, that** Spokes ~~come next, making~~ **that make** the web resemble an

old-fashioned wagon wheel, and finally, ~~the spinning of~~

crosslines **that** connect ~~s~~ the spokes tightly**, and make the web strong.** ~~These give the web~~

~~its strength.~~ Spiders are good engineers ~~with built-in skill at~~

and designers, patient hunters, and resilient creatures that
~~designing. They hunt really patiently, too. If no prey arrives~~

~~immediately, the spider will wait. In addition, the spider has~~

they have
~~resilience. It~~ can go without food a long time if ~~it has~~ water.

©2009. Allyn & Bacon, a division of Pearson Education. Developed by Vicki Spandel. All rights reserved.

Sample C: Whole Class Revision

Parallel
Structure?

Rats are survivors. Several characteristics have made this

easier. A rat is very flexible, and can collapse its body to a

much smaller size, allowing it to squeeze into small spaces.

It has powerful jaws, and can bite right through almost

anything (even concrete). In addition, their sense of touch is

quite remarkable, and this lets a rat retrace its steps when

hunting food or seeking shelter. Perhaps the characteristic

that has kept the rat alive through thousands of years and in

countless different cultures is its adaptability. The rat will

eat virtually anything that does not eat it first. It will

consume garbage of all varieties, no matter how disgusting.

Rats have been known to eat rice, steak, or veggies that

might be leftovers. Small prey, such as birds or rodents,

may even be hunted. For the rat, a picnic is never far away.

©2009. Allyn & Bacon, a division of Pearson Education. Developed by Vicki Spandel. All rights reserved.

Sample D: Revising with Partners

Parallel
Structure?

If you're considering traveling—such as taking a vacation,

or let's say you like to camp, or you might be headed across

town—it is a good idea to take a first aid kit with you. If

you plan to be gone overnight, of course, you'll want

prescription medications with you. But there are other

everyday things you might not think of without a list. They

are simple things. But they are important, too. Consider

taking some bandages and scissors in case of an injury. Pain

killers are another good idea because they reduce pain and

can thin the blood in case of a heart attack or stroke. It's

always good to take antibiotic cream, which is useful in the

event of a cut or scratch. Having a good first aid kit with

you can make you feel safe. It gives you a kind of

confidence, too. It makes you feel that just in case

something unexpected were to happen, you would be ready.

©2009. Allyn & Bacon, a division of Pearson Education. Developed by Vicki Spandel. All rights reserved.

Suggested Revisions of C and D

Sample C: Whole Class Revision

Rats are survivors. Several characteristics have made this

easier. A rat ~~is very~~ *has a* flexible, ~~and can collapse its~~ *collapsible* body ~~to a~~

~~much smaller size~~ allowing it to squeeze into small spaces.

~~It has~~ powerful jaws, ~~and~~ *that* can bite right through almost

anything (even concrete). ~~In addition, their~~ *and a remarkable* sense of touch

~~is quite remarkable, and this~~ *that* lets a rat retrace its steps when

hunting food or seeking shelter. Perhaps the characteristic

that has kept the rat alive through thousands of years and in

countless different cultures is its adaptability. The rat will

eat virtually anything that does not eat it first. ~~It will~~

~~consume~~ garbage, *including the most disgusting* ~~of all varieties, no matter how disgusting~~

~~Rats have been known to eat~~ *leftover* rice, steak, or veggies, ~~that~~

~~might be leftovers.~~ *and even* Small prey, such as birds or rodents.

~~may even be hunted.~~ For the rat, a picnic is never far away.

©2009. Allyn & Bacon, a division of Pearson Education. Developed by Vicki Spandel. All rights reserved.

Sample D: Revising with Partners

If you're considering traveling—~~such as~~ _whether you are_ taking a vacation, ~~or let's say you like to camp,~~ _going camping,_ or ~~you might be headed~~ _simply heading_ across

town—it is a good idea to take a first aid kit with you. If

you plan to be gone overnight, of course, you'll want

prescription medications with you. But there are other

everyday things, _(simple things, important things,)_ you might not think of without a list. ~~They are simple things. But they are important, too.~~ Consider

taking some bandages and scissors in case of an injury.

_to_ ~~Pain killers are another good idea because they~~ reduce pain

and ~~can~~ thin the blood in case of a heart attack or stroke.

and ~~It's always good to take~~ antibiotic cream, which is useful in

case ~~the event~~ of a cut or scratch. Having a good first aid kit with

you can make you feel safe. ~~It gives you a kind of~~

confident, and prepared. ~~confidence, too. It makes you feel that just in case~~

~~something unexpected were to happen, you would be ready.~~

©2009. Allyn & Bacon, a division of Pearson Education. Developed by Vicki Spandel. All rights reserved.

Confusing Little Words

Trait Connection: **Conventions**

Introduction (Read aloud or share with students in your own words.)

The last editing lesson dealt with *lie* and *lay*—words often confused in English. In this lesson, we'll take on a new batch of confusing words. They're words you likely use in speaking and writing all the time, and we'll look at them set by set. They are—

- *accept, except*
- *all ready, already*
- *all together, altogether*
- *principal, principle*

On the following page is a chart to guide you through the differences. Take a close look at the examples. Ask someone in your class to read the example sentences aloud. Try to get a picture of the word in your mind as you listen. You may also wish to make up a sentence of your own using each word.

(*Note to teacher:* The chart and warm-up samples are on a separate page so that you can use them as a handout, if you wish.)

Confusing Words Chart

The word	Means	Example
accept	take	***Accept*** my apology.
except	but	I want all the burger toppings ***except*** onions.
all ready	totally prepared	We were ***all ready*** for the party.
already	before	Jason ***already*** left!
all together	everyone at once	***All together*** now, let's cheer!
altogether	entirely	That is ***altogether*** different.
principal	head of school	Ms. Dixon is our ***principal.***
principal	main	What is the ***principal*** idea here?
principle	rule, ethic	He has strong ***principles***.

Warm-Up

Let's warm up. For each of the following sentences, choose the right form of the word. Look back at the chart to help you, if you wish:

I cannot (accept / except) **this money.**

Everyone (accept / except) **Sharon loved the film.**

Are you (already / all ready)**?**

I bought eggs (already / all ready)**—now we have four dozen!**

Let's do this (all together / altogether)**, as a team should.**

Diving is (all together / altogether) **different from swimming.**

The (principal / principle) **loves visiting our classroom.**

My (principal / principle) **reason for coming was to see you.**

The (principals / principles) **of grammar often escape me.**

Answers to Warm-Up

I cannot <u>accept</u> this money.

Everyone <u>except</u> Sharon loved the film.

Are you <u>all ready</u>?

I bought eggs <u>already</u>—now we have four dozen!

Let's do this <u>all together</u>, as a team should.

Diving is <u>altogether</u> different from swimming.

The <u>principal</u> loves to visit our classroom.

My <u>principal</u> reason for coming was to see you.

The <u>principles</u> of grammar often escape me.

If you had any difficulty with that warm-up, take another look at the chart, and try writing a sentence using each word you still find confusing. Then repeat the warm-up. By then, you should be all ready for the editing lesson, which is all about the principles of careful word choice. You and your classmates will do it all together, except that you'll be working principally with one partner. It's an altogether fascinating lesson—so accept the challenge!

Teaching the Lesson (General Guidelines for Teachers)

1. Share the examples above, making the chart available to students as a reference.

2. Answer any questions, providing additional practice as necessary.

3. Share the editing lesson on the following page. Students should read the passage silently, correcting words that are wrong (7). *Some (3) are right <u>as is</u>.*

4. Ask them to edit individually first, then check with a partner. Some students find it helpful to underline each word in question first, then make a decision, referring to the chart as they go.

5. When everyone is done, ask them to coach you as you edit the same copy.

6. When you finish, read your edited copy aloud, taking time to discuss reasons behind each choice. Compare your edited copy with our suggested text on page 218.

Editing Goal: Correct 7 errors involving confusing words.
Follow-Up: Review your own writing to make sure you have used the correct forms of words reviewed in this lesson.

Editing Practice

Use the correct form of each word:
- **accept/except**
- **already/all ready**
- **altogether/all together**
- **principal/principle**

It was already 7 a.m. Susan Doyle, principle of New Heights School, was late for the pep rally. Her speech was already—except that she still had to get there to give it. It would be great, she thought, to see the students altogether, cheering for their football team. They had not lost a game yet. It had been an all together spectacular season. Today would be the moment everyone had waited for—when the football captain and coach each got to except an achievement award. This was her principle reason for wanting to make the opening speech. Dedication and hard work were principals she believed in, right down to her toes. It was altogether fitting that she be the one to hand out this award.

©2009. Allyn & Bacon, a division of Pearson Education. Developed by Vicki Spandel. All rights reserved.

Edited Copy

Correct forms inserted in place of 7 misused words:
- **accept/except**
- **already/all ready**
- **altogether/all together**
- **principal/principle**

3 correct usages are <u>underlined</u> **for easy reference.**

It was <u>already</u> 7 a.m. Susan Doyle, ~~principle~~ **principal** of New

Heights School, was late for the pep rally. Her speech was

~~already~~ **all ready**—<u>except</u> that she still had to get there to give it. It

would be great, she thought, to see the students ~~altogether~~ **all together,**

cheering for their football team. They had not lost a game

yet. It had been an ~~all together~~ **altogether** spectacular season. Today

would be the moment everyone had waited for—when the

football captain and coach each got to ~~except~~ **accept** an achievement

award. This was her ~~principle~~ **principal** reason for wanting to make

the opening speech. Dedication and hard work were

~~principals~~ **principles** she believed in, right down to her toes. It was

<u>altogether</u> fitting that she be the one to hand out this award.

©2009. Allyn & Bacon, a division of Pearson Education. Developed by Vicki Spandel. All rights reserved.

Revising with Repetition

Trait Connection: **Sentence Fluency**

Introduction

You have likely heard—more than once—that one key to sentence fluency is to begin your sentences in a variety of ways. That is still good advice. Every now and then, however, good writers break the so-called "rules" of writing—if they have a good reason. While mindless repetition of the same sentence beginning (*Rex is my friend. Rex can run the mile faster than anyone. Rex is the funniest guy I know . . .*) is nothing more than an annoyance, *purposeful* repetition is another thing entirely. Through purposeful repetition, a writer can create a rhetorical rhythm. Like a verbal drumbeat, deliberate repetition of a key word or phrase appeals to the human ear. It says to the reader, "Pay attention. Tune in. I *mean* this." As with any special strategy that does not follow the norm, it's important not to overdo it. Be selective. Repeat what matters. Like an echo in a canyon, verbal repetition is attention-getting at first. But no one wants *every word* echoed.

Teacher's Sidebar . . .

It is fun to experiment with rules from time to time, creating special effects. This lesson allows for that, but also serves as a reminder that rule breaking works best when it is purposeful. Accidental repetition that the writer does not intend is rarely successful. Purposeful repetition, by contrast, is one of the strongest rhetorical strategies a writer can use. Repetition can involve just one word, a phrase, or a whole sentence. Short repetition can come at the beginning, middle, or end of a sentence. The more you experiment, the more fun—and success—you will have with this lesson.

Focus and Intent

This lesson is intended to help students:

- Understand the rhetorical power of purposeful repetition.
- Recognize repetition that works—and repetition that does not.
- Revise a piece by rewording sentences to eliminate ineffective repetition, and inserting purposeful repetition for rhetorical emphasis.

Teaching the Lesson

Step 1: Hearing It Again . . . and Again

Repeating words or phrases is no *guarantee* of rhetorical effectiveness. You have to ask, "Does this repetition work? Do I like the *sound* of it?" Read the following examples aloud, more than once. Put a check beside those in which the repetition works. For those where it does not work, revise to eliminate the repetition—or change it, if you prefer. The first two are done for you. (Notice the addition of repetition in Sample 2.)

✓ 1. Elsa stared at the horizon. She stared from the moment it became visible until long after the sun was up. She stared until her eyes stung and tears flowed. She did not move. She did not look away. And finally she saw what she'd been waiting for: a tiny moving speck that was, *had* to be, her son.

___ 2. Raul woke up early. He slipped into his uniform. He went downstairs. He had a quick breakfast. Then he bolted out the door. Raul knew this would be a big day for him.

Raul woke up early, slipped into his uniform, grabbed a quick breakfast and bolted out the door. This would be a big day for him. A very big day.

___ 3. Why was she the only one of her friends who had to be home by 9 sharp? Why was she the only one who couldn't have a dog? Why was her house the only one that had to have all the beds made and the carpets vacuumed by 10 a.m.? *Why?* That's what Kirsten wanted to know.

___ 4. The math test was the reason Owen couldn't sleep at night. The math test was the reason he had precisely zero nanoseconds of free time. The math test was the reason his mom thought he "probably shouldn't" go to a friend's house or the movies or have a semi-normal life. The math test was ruining *everything*.

___ 5. It was the last game of the summer season, and that was a good thing, Tiger thought. It was getting hot to be running bases or standing out in center field. It was not as if Tiger got up to bat a lot. It was not the most exciting season he could recall.

Step 2: Making the Reading-Writing Connection

In *Lizzie Bright and the Buckminster Boy*, the two lead characters, Turner and Lizzie, are developing a secret friendship—a friendship of which Turner's family would not approve. They meet at a beach where Lizzie comes to dig clams; it's a place where they can be alone to talk and think. Listen for the repetition of one phrase that tells us how the two friends feel about this time and place:

Blue days, as the tide washed away the twin footprints Lizzie and Turner left along the beach . . . Blue days, as they sprinted against the sea breeze and chased the gulls until Turner finally, finally, finally touched a tail feather. Blue days, as they dangled their legs over the granite ledge and felt the gigantic continent beneath them.

(From Gary D. Schmidt. *Lizzie Bright and the Buckminster Boy.* 2004. New York: Clarion. Page 73.)

Have you had "blue days" of your own, of the sort described in this scene? Imagine that author Gary D. Schmidt had used the expression "blue days" only one time. What would be lost? Notice the other instance of repetition in this passage. What is its impact?

Step 3: Involving Students as Evaluators

Ask students to review Samples A and B, particularly looking and listening for repetition. Have students work with a partner, thinking about whether each writer uses repetition and whether that repetition is effective. Encourage students to underline repeated words or phrases and to write their personal responses to that repetition in the margin.

Discussing Results

Most students should identify Sample B as more effective. The writer of Sample A uses repetition, to be sure, but the result seems more accidental than purposeful. One possible revision of Sample B is provided. You may wish to ask students to discuss revision possibilities prior to sharing our example.

Step 4: Modeling Revision

- Share Sample C (*Whole Class Revision*) with students. Read it aloud, looking and listening for examples of repetition.

- Talk about whether the writer of Sample C has used repetition (*yes*) and whether such repetition is effective. (Most students should say *no*.) Invite students to coach you through a class revision, discussing when and where repetition might be effective—and where it should probably be eliminated. Revise accordingly.

- When you finish, read through the entire piece, listening to the rhetorical effectiveness of the repetition you have used. Does it create emphasis, an effective echo, without going too far? If you wish, compare your revision with ours, remembering that our decision regarding when and how to use repetition may or may not match yours.

Step 5: Revising with Partners

Share copies of Sample D (*Revising with Partners*). Ask students to follow the basic steps you modeled with Sample C. *Working with partners,* they should:

- Read the piece aloud, asking themselves whether the author has used repetition, and if so, whether it works.
- Discuss when and where purposeful repetition might occur.
- Revise accordingly—remembering to experiment and test different options.
- Read the final draft aloud, beginning to end, to listen for rhetorical effectiveness.

Step 6: Sharing and Discussing Results

When students have finished, ask several pairs of students to share their revisions aloud. Did teams tend to repeat the same words and phrases? Did some use more repetition than others? Compare your final draft with ours if you wish, noting that we may have used more repetition for purposes of modeling.

Next Steps

- Ask students to review their own writing for *non-deliberate* repetition (it helps to highlight the first four words of each sentence) and to revise by (1) rewording sentences so that most beginnings vary, and/or (2) occasionally incorporating *purposeful* repetition to emphasize an important idea.

- In response groups, students can support one another by listening to recordings of brief passages and asking whether repetition is a purposeful echo or an accident.

- Listen for repetition in the literature you share with students. Save favorite moments, and post them as models. Recommended:
  - *Lizzie Bright and the Buckminster Boy* by Gary D. Schmidt. 2006. New York: Yearling.
  - *Dogteam* by Gary Paulsen. 1995. New York: Dragonfly Books.
  - *The House on Mango Street* by Sandra Cisneros. 1991. New York: Vintage.
  - *Maniac Magee* by Jerry Spinelli. 2002. New York: Scholastic.

- *For an additional challenge:* Rhetorical repetition can be particularly effective in persuasive writing. Ask students to draft a persuasive paragraph on any issue about which they have strong feelings, and to use repetition to emphasize a key theme of their argument. Read results aloud—and talk about how slogans sometimes evolve from such repetition.

Sample A

Persuasive Essay on Global Warming

Effective echoes? or mindless repetition?

Global warming is one of the most serious issues of our time. Global warming could affect virtually every country on earth, and our entire way of life. Global warming is partly a natural phenomenon. Most scientists believe, however, that it is caused, to some extent, by carbon dioxide emissions—the cumulative effects of industry and automobile emissions. Global warming seems to occur slowly—with average temperatures rising only about one degree every hundred years or so. Even a small temperature rise, however, can have startling impact. Global warming, according to some scientists, is causing melting of the polar ice caps. This in turn could lead to a rise in sea levels, the extinction of some species—such as the polar bear and types of penguins, and severe weather patterns. Global warming is an issue we cannot afford to ignore.

©2009. Allyn & Bacon, a division of Pearson Education. Developed by Vicki Spandel. All rights reserved.

Sample B

Persuasive Essay on Wetlands

Effective echoes? Or mindless repetition?

A wetlands is more than a swamp. Much more. When we think swamp, we think muck. We think bog. We think of dampness and drizzle and low clouds and fog and unsavory odors. We think of sinking up to our boot tops in mud. But a wetlands is more than a swamp. It is in fact a home for a spectacularly diverse array of plants, birds, amphibians, reptiles, and small mammals—many of which cannot live *anywhere* else. It is a barrier between dry land and deeper water, and as such, it provides protective flood control. It is a biological factory that works day and night to clean the waters that enter it. It is a recreational area, valued for its beauty. It is a place to observe wildlife, to take breathtaking photographs, and to fish. It is a breeding ground for many edible creatures we enjoy on our dinner tables, such as shrimp. Before you think about draining a wetlands to make room for a shopping center no one needs, remember: a wetlands is more than a swamp. Much more.

©2009. Allyn & Bacon, a division of Pearson Education. Developed by Vicki Spandel. All rights reserved.

Suggested Revision of Sample A

Persuasive Essay on
Global Warming

Global warming, is one of the most serious issues of our time. Global
warming could affect virtually every country on earth, and our entire
way of life. Global warming is partly a natural phenomenon, most
scientists believe, however, that it is caused, to some extent, by carbon
dioxide emissions—the cumulative effects of industry and automobile
emissions. Global warming seems to occur slowly—with average
temperatures rising only about one degree every hundred years or so.

Even a small temperature rise, however, can have startling impact.

Global warming, according to some scientists, is causing melting of
Even a small temperature rise can melt
the polar ice caps. This in turn could lead to a rise in sea levels.
Even a small temperature rise can raise sea levels and hasten
the extinction of some species—such as the polar bear and types of
Even a small temperature rise can create
penguins, and severe weather patterns. Global warming is an issue we
cannot afford to ignore.

©2009. Allyn & Bacon, a division of Pearson Education. Developed by Vicki Spandel. All rights reserved.

Sample C: Whole Class Revision

Lost

Effective echoes?
or mindless
repetition?

It was more than four hours since Zeke had split up from his camping buddies. He had wanted to explore the dunes, and he'd believed it was a fairly small area, that getting lost would be impossible—unless you were a total dork with no sense of direction whatsoever. Which Zeke was *not*. He wished very much that he had brought his compass with him. In addition, it would be really good to have something to eat. He was hungry. He was also cold— and the sun was sinking lower by the minute. He had not thought to bring a decent jacket with him. He was all by himself, too. He should probably have stayed with the group. He was pretty sure someone would find him eventually—but what if it took a couple of days?

©2009. Allyn & Bacon, a division of Pearson Education. Developed by Vicki Spandel. All rights reserved.

Sample D: Revising with Partners

Bad Luck

Effective echoes?
or mindless
repetition?

Lauren wasn't sure she liked her after-school job all that much. She felt lucky to have a job. She liked making some money. She knew a lot of her friends had not found a job. She wished she could have found something different, however. It was just rotten luck. She didn't like having to work outside in the rain. She also didn't like having to push heavy shopping carts around. She especially disliked working for someone who never smiled. Never! *Everybody smiles once in a while*, she thought, if only by accident.

She was sinking deeper into this pit of self-pity when something amazing happened. She spotted her best friend, Jennifer, pushing a long line of shopping carts through the parking lot. She hadn't known Jennifer worked at the same place! She realized her bad luck was turning!

©2009. Allyn & Bacon, a division of Pearson Education. Developed by Vicki Spandel. All rights reserved.

Suggested Revisions of C and D

Sample C: Whole Class Revision

Lost

It was more than four hours since Zeke had split up from

his camping buddies. He had wanted to explore the dunes,

and he'd believed it was a fairly small area, that getting lost

would be impossible—unless you were a total dork with no

sense of direction whatsoever. Which Zeke was *not*. He

wished very much that he had brought his compass with

(He wished he had something)

him. ~~In addition, it would be~~ really good ~~to have something~~

He wished—with

to eat. ~~He was hungry. He was also cold—and~~ the sun ~~was~~

—he had

sinking lower by the minute. ~~He had not~~ thought to bring a

(wished he had had the good sense to stay)

decent jacket with him. He ~~was all by himself, too. He~~

(Wishes wouldn't get him rescued, however.)

~~should probably have stayed~~ with the group. He was pretty

sure someone would find him eventually—but what if it

took a couple of days?

©2009. Allyn & Bacon, a division of Pearson Education. Developed by Vicki Spandel. All rights reserved.

Sample D: Revising with Partners

Rotten
~~Bad~~ Luck

Lauren wasn't sure she liked her after-school job all that

when so many of her friends hadn't found one. It was good to be

much. She felt lucky to have a job. ~~She liked~~ making some

money. ~~She knew a lot of her friends had not found a job~~

She wished she could have found something different,

Rotten luck

however. It was just rotten luck. ~~She didn't like~~ having to

Rotten luck

work outside in the rain. ~~She also didn't like~~ having to push

Especially rotten luck

heavy shopping carts around. ~~She especially disliked~~

working for someone who never smiled. Never! *Everybody*

smiles once in a while, she thought, if only by accident.

She was sinking deeper into this pit of self-pity when

~~something amazing happened~~ She spotted her best friend,

Jennifer, pushing a long line of shopping carts through the

Could it be that   was working

parking lot. ~~She hadn't known~~ Jennifer ~~worked~~ at the same

Maybe Lauren's rotten

place? ~~She realized her bad~~ luck was turning!

©2009. Allyn & Bacon, a division of Pearson Education. Developed by Vicki Spandel. All rights reserved.

Avoiding Double Negatives

Trait Connection: **Conventions**

Introduction (Read aloud or share with students in your own words.)

In math, we learn that two negatives, multiplied, result in a *positive*. But in writing, two negatives result in a nonstandard expression—such as one of these:

There <u>weren't</u> <u>no</u> more apples in the pantry.

We <u>hadn't</u> <u>never</u> gone swimming by ourselves.

There <u>wasn't</u> <u>no one</u> left on the field.

It <u>hadn't</u> <u>scarcely</u> started raining, but we left anyway.

<u>Neither</u> choice <u>wasn't</u> acceptable.

He <u>wasn't</u> <u>no</u> thief, that's for sure.

Here are the correct versions of these sentences:

There **weren't any** more apples in the pantry.

We **hadn't ever** gone swimming by ourselves.

There **wasn't anyone** left on the field.

It **had scarcely** started raining, but we left anyway.

Neither choice **was** acceptable.

He **was no** thief, that's for sure.

On the following page is a list of frequently used negative words, and a warm-up to let you practice changing **double negatives** to **single negatives**.

(*Note to teacher:* The list and warm-up samples are on a separate page so that you can use them as a handout, if you wish.)

List of Common Negatives (Don't double up!)

-n't (any contraction ending in *-n't*, which stands for *not*)

scarcely (This word, meaning *hardly*, functions as a negative)

hardly (Same as *scarcely*)

neither

never

no

no one

none

nobody

not

nothing

nowhere

Warm-Up

Correct each sentence to eliminate the double negative. Work with a partner.

I couldn't hardly say no to his invitation

She wouldn't never tell a lie.

My cat wasn't nowhere to be found.

I was happy to do it. It wasn't nothing.

That option wasn't never considered.

I wasn't hardly done with my homework when he called.

He wasn't nobody you would think of as a great actor.

Nobody scarcely showed up for the meeting.

There wasn't hardly nothing left of the snow by noon.

Answers to Warm-Up

I **could** hardly say no to his invitation. (OR, *I couldn't say no . . .*)

She wouldn't **ever** tell a lie. (OR, *She would never . . .*)

My cat **was** nowhere to be found. (OR, *My cat wasn't anywhere . . .*)

I was happy to do it. It **was** nothing. (OR, *It wasn't anything . . .*)

That option wasn't **ever** considered. (OR, *. . . was never considered*)

I **was** hardly done with my homework when he called.

He wasn't **anybody** you would think of as a great actor. (OR, *he was nobody . . .*)

Scarcely **anyone** showed up for the meeting. (OR, *almost nobody . . .*)

There **was** hardly **anything** left of the snow by noon. (OR, *There wasn't anything . . .*)

You may have noticed that there is usually more than one way to correct a double negative. For example, ***It wasn't nothing*** might become

It <u>was</u> nothing, or

It wasn't <u>anything</u>.

Either is correct. The lesson that follows contains several double negatives. Correct all of them, using the list of common negatives and the warm-up as guides.

Teaching the Lesson (General Guidelines for Teachers)

1. Share the examples above, making the list of negatives available to students as a reference.

2. Share the editing lesson on the following page. Students should read the passage carefully, correcting all double negatives.

3. Ask them to edit individually first, then check with a partner.

4. When everyone is done, ask them to coach you as you edit the same copy.

5. When you finish, read your edited copy aloud, taking time to discuss reasons behind each change. (Remember, there is more than one way to correct most double negatives.) Compare your edited copy with our suggested text on page 234.

Editing Goal: Correct 6 double negatives.
Follow-Up: Watch for (and correct) double negatives in your own writing.

Editing Practice

Correct all double negatives.

It wasn't hardly fair! Jasper was the one who didn't never want to race, and now he was calling Ernie a coward. Ernie had never been called a coward in his whole life. Everyone was betting on Jasper to win. It didn't hardly make any sense. Jasper wasn't someone you would think of as an athlete. He hadn't never run track or anything. He wasn't really a very competitive person neither. But now here they were, about to race cross country for four miles. Ernie was determined to win, no matter what it took. Maybe he wasn't the fastest runner in his class, but there wasn't no one who could get by with calling him a coward. He was a competitor. That was that.

©2009. Allyn & Bacon, a division of Pearson Education. Developed by Vicki Spandel. All rights reserved.

Edited Copy

6 double negatives corrected (corrections are numbered)

was (1)
It ~~wasn't~~ hardly fair! Jasper was the one who didn't ~~never~~ **ever (2)**

want to race, and now he was calling Ernie a coward. Ernie

had never been called a coward in his whole life. Everyone

(3)
was betting on Jasper to win. It didn't ~~hardly~~ make any

sense. Jasper wasn't someone you would think of as an

had (4)
athlete. He ~~hadn't~~ never run track or anything. He wasn't

either. (5)
really a very competitive person ~~neither~~ But now here they

were, about to race cross country for four miles. Ernie was

determined to win, no matter what it took. Maybe he wasn't

anyone (6)
the fastest runner in his class, but there wasn't ~~no one~~ who

could get by with calling him a coward. He was a

competitor. That was that.

©2009. Allyn & Bacon, a division of Pearson Education. Developed by Vicki Spandel. All rights reserved.

Revising Dialogue with Tension

Trait Connection: **Sentence Fluency**

Introduction

Interesting dialogue exists to reveal something about one or both characters, create a particular mood (humorous, hostile, suspenseful, etc.), or advance the plot in some way. None of these things can happen if characters are forever saying things like, "Hello. My name is Paul" or "Pass the milk," or "What shall we do today?" Writers can put a little tension into dialogue by having characters disagree, get themselves into (or out of) trouble, reveal a surprise, or show their inner feelings. Tension doesn't always imply hostility. Think of tension as the creation of built-up energy, like stretching a rubber band. Sooner or later, you'll have to let go—and something exciting is bound to happen when you do.

Teacher's Sidebar . . .

Revising dialogue sometimes takes bold strokes. When the writer changes what *one* person says, the other character's previous response may no longer make sense. So encourage students to first think about who the people in each scenario really are. What are they thinking? Will they let the other person in on what they're thinking—or try to hide it in some way? Do they like each other? Do they agree? How are they feeling—happy, angry, excited, fearful? The objective is to show who they are, to make them real and human. That may require revising virtually *everything* they say to each other.

Focus and Intent

This lesson is intended to help students:

- Understand the power of strong dialogue.
- Distinguish between strong dialogue and dialogue that goes nowhere.
- Strengthen a piece by revising the dialogue to give it tension.

Teaching the Lesson

Step 1: Stretching the Rubber Band

Following are several sets of dialogue in which you'll hear from both speakers once. Read each set aloud, with a different person performing each part, as if it were out of a stage play. Put a check by the examples you feel have tension—the dialogue that is *going somewhere*.

____ **Toby**: *I'm asking you for the last time. Get off the boat.*
Derek: *And I'm telling you for the last time. I don't swim!*

____ **Ana**: *Would you like soup or a sandwich for lunch?*
Felice: *I like them both. You decide.*

____ **Roger**: *Something about that guy looks so familiar . . .*
Maria: *Your imagination's playing tricks on you.*

____ **Carlos**: *What's in the box?*
Alonso: *You don't want to know.*

____ **C. J.**: *Let's go to the movies.*
Chris: *That is a good idea. What would you like to see?*

That was probably fairly simple, right? Let's add a bit of a challenge. For each dialogue set you checked, try writing the next two lines, one line for each character. (You can divide the class into three groups, working on one dialogue set each, to make this go faster.) Then, look at the dialogue sets you said were going nowhere. Leave the first line as is, but have the second person respond in a way that puts some tension into the conversation. *Hint: The more unexpected the response, the more tension you'll create.*

Step 2: Making the Reading-Writing Connection

In *No More Dead Dogs*, the main character Wallace Wallace is given detention for turning in a negative but honest book report on a book he hates—*Old Shep, My Pal*. Detention is held in the auditorium, where the class is rehearsing a production of "Old Shep, My Pal"—and the play is, if anything, schmaltzier (*more disgustingly sentimental*) than the book. While Mr. Fogelman (English teacher turned director) defends the play, Wallace maintains that no live, breathing, real human being would utter a line as phony as "Great heavens, this dog has suffered an injury." Before he knows it, he's found himself in the position of revising:

> *"Okay, it may be a little old-fashioned," Mr. Fogelman admitted. "The book was published in 1951. Besides, what's he supposed to say? We have to let the audience know he's found the dog."*
>
> *Wallace shrugged. "Not 'Great heavens.' How about something normal like 'Hey!' or 'Look at this!' or even 'Check it out!'? That's how people talk."*

(From Gordon Korman. *No More Dead Dogs*. 2000. New York: Hyperion. Pages 34–35.)

Do you agree with Wallace Wallace that the original line—"Great heavens, this dog has suffered an injury"—is a little phony sounding? How do you like Wallace's alternatives? Imagine you are in the position of rewriting the play. What dialogue might you put into the scene where the characters discover that Old Shep has been struck by a car? Notice that author Gordon Korman is doing something very tricky here. He's writing a comic novel about a supposedly serious play, and creating dialogue *about* dialogue. That's a challenge. To get a more complete sense of this very funny scene, check out pages 34–37 of the book.

Step 3: Involving Students as Evaluators

Ask students to review Samples A and B, particularly looking at and listening to the dialogue. Have students work with a partner, thinking about whether each set of dialogue creates tension that contributes to character development, plot, or mood. Encourage students to underline or highlight any dialogue they feel sounds stiff or artificial, and to make marginal notes about how it might be revised.

Discussing Results

Most students should identify Sample A as more effective. The writer of Sample A uses dialogue to help us understand the characters, and to create a feeling of suspense. The dialogue in Sample B, by contrast, does not sound as if it were spoken by real human beings—and yet there is real opportunity for tension in this situation. One possible revision of Sample B is provided. You may wish to ask students to discuss revision possibilities prior to sharing our example.

Step 4: Modeling Revision

- Share Sample C (*Whole Class Revision*) with students. Read it aloud, possibly with two readers.

- Talk about whether the dialogue in Sample C bristles with tension, or collapses under its own phoniness. (Most students should say *there is little to no tension.*) Invite students to coach you through a class revision, discussing the kinds of changes that will bring this flat dialogue between Paul and his dad to life. Revise accordingly.

- When you finish, read through the entire piece (in two voices, if you wish), listening to the new dialogue. Does it create tension that will keep a reader guessing what Paul will decide to do? If you wish, compare your revision with ours, remembering that our revision is unlikely to match yours in any way—particularly because each new line of dialogue opens a completely different array of possibilities.

Step 5: Revising with Partners

Share copies of Sample D (*Revising with Partners*). Ask students to follow the basic steps you modeled with Sample C. *Working with partners,* they should:

- Read the piece aloud, asking themselves whether the author has used dialogue to advance the plot, reveal character, or create mood.

- Discuss ways of adding more tension to the existing dialogue.

- Revise accordingly—remembering to test each revision by reading aloud—and using two voices.

- Read the final draft aloud, beginning to end, listening for authenticity and tension in the dialogue.

Step 6: Sharing and Discussing Results

When students have finished, ask several pairs of students to share their revisions aloud, reading in two voices. Did teams create very different dialogue sets? Which teams injected the most tension between Lacey and Harris? Compare your final draft with ours if you wish, noting that our revisions are unlikely to correspond to yours, but may still be compared in terms of authenticity and tension.

Next Steps

- Characters come to life when we hear them speak. Remind students of the importance of dialogue in making any narrative or character sketch authentic. In an informational or persuasive piece, a short anecdote involving dialogue makes a powerful introduction or conclusion.

- In response groups, invite student writers to share one key line of dialogue, and ask listeners to write a possible response on a 3x5 card. Turn them all in to the writer, who can read them aloud to the group, and compare listeners' speculations to the actual dialogue. Which has more tension? More authenticity?

- Listen for good dialogue in the literature you share with students. Perform some of it to get the full effect. Recommended:
  - *No More Dead Dogs* by Gordon Korman. 2000. New York: Hyperion.
  - *Dovey Coe* by Frances O'Roark Dowell. 2001. New York: Aladdin.
  - *Holes* by Louis Sachar. 2003. New York: Yearling.
  - *Jack's Black Book* by Jack Gantos. 1997. New York: Farrar, Straus, and Giroux.

- *For an additional challenge:* Take any fairy tale, fable, or chapter from a longer work and rewrite it as a play for two, three, or four voices (feeling free to tweak the plot slightly, of course). Rehearse until each character's speech has just the right amount of tension. Then perform it for the class.

Sample A

Tension?
Authenticity?

Karim's parents had left to pick up his adopted baby sister, Deborah. Karim waited with his Aunt Esther, who flitted about the kitchen, preparing tea, cakes, rice, and fruit as if this were the event of the century. "Why are you looking so glum?" she asked, noticing Karim's expression and dark eyes for the first time.

"I am not looking *glum*," he replied. "I am trying to look *invisible*—which is what I am about to become."

"That's not *true*," Aunt Esther responded, hugging Karim, and tenderly brushing the thick black hair from his face. He wasn't always open to affection, but this time he didn't shrug off her attention with a laugh, as he usually did. "You will *always* be visible to me. And now, with the baby, you'll be *more* important than ever to your mother."

Karim looked at his aunt intently, and when he spoke, it was very soft. "I have *never* been important—not to anyone but you. And soon, not even you will pay attention. Watch. One day, I'll slip away, and no one will see me go—or think to look for me." Before Esther could protest, Karim was out the door.

©2009. Allyn & Bacon, a division of Pearson Education. Developed by Vicki Spandel. All rights reserved.

Sample B

Tension?
Authenticity?

At age 13, Frances had a shot at having a children's book published. Who in the real world *did that?* Molly couldn't help feeling jealous. She was a better writer than Queen Fran any day, but she couldn't very well say *that*. She would have to lie . . .

"That is good news, Fran."

"Thank you, Molly! I hope they choose my book."

"Do you think they will?" Molly could not believe her ears. The Queen, not being the chosen one? How could it be?

"They might not," Fran said, looking worried.

Molly hated herself for being happy that her best friend might fail at something—but she couldn't seem to help it. She did her best to cover up the smile spreading across her face.

"I think they will like your book," she said, smiling. "It is very good." Molly wasn't about to admit that she hadn't actually read even one page.

"Molly, you are a fine friend," Fran said.

©2009. Allyn & Bacon, a division of Pearson Education. Developed by Vicki Spandel. All rights reserved.

Suggested Revision of Sample B

At age 13, Frances had a shot at having a children's book published. Who in the real world *did that?* Molly couldn't help feeling jealous. She was a better writer than Queen Fran any day, but she couldn't very well say *that*. She would have to lie . . .

"Way to go, Fran. You're amazing!"
~~"That is good news, Fran."~~

"Yeah, I *guess* . . . But what if they don't choose my book?"
~~"Thank you, Molly! I hope they choose my book."~~

"Don't be ridiculous! Why the heck wouldn't they choose it?"
~~"Do you think they will?"~~ Molly could not believe her ears. The Queen, not being the chosen one? How could it be?

"I don't know. But I think I'll *die* if this book doesn't get published,"   **as if she might burst into tears at any minute.**
~~"They might not."~~ Fran said, looking ~~worried~~.

Molly hated herself for being happy that her best friend might fail at something—but she couldn't seem to help it. She did her best to cover up the smile spreading across her face.

"Don't be crazy—they're going to LOVE it, Frannie,"
~~"I think they will like your book,"~~ she said, smiling. ~~"It is very~~

"It's absolutely the best thing I've read in my whole life!"
~~good."~~ Molly wasn't about to admit that she hadn't actually read even one page.

"I'm giving you an autographed copy of my book,"
~~"Molly, you are a fine friend,"~~ Fran said.
Luckily, she did not see the look on Molly's face.

©2009. Allyn & Bacon, a division of Pearson Education. Developed by Vicki Spandel. All rights reserved.

Sample C: Whole Class Revision

Tension?
Authenticity?

Every single day of his life, Paul wished his family lived in the city. His friends all thought it was so great living on a farm. Let them try it on chicken butchering day. That was enough to cure anyone of romantic notions about farm life, Paul figured.

"Come on, Paul," his dad said, grabbing some gloves and heading for the chicken pen. "This is a hard task."

"Yes, it is," Paul answered.

"It's a good thing I have you to help," his dad added, ignoring Paul's lack of enthusiasm.

"I would prefer not to participate," Paul replied—at which point his dad looked very puzzled.

"It is not anyone's favorite task," he said. "But butchering a chicken will give us something good to eat."

Paul shrugged. "Perhaps we could buy our chicken from the store," he suggested. "Those chickens are not pets."

©2009. Allyn & Bacon, a division of Pearson Education. Developed by Vicki Spandel. All rights reserved.

Sample D: Revising with Partners

Tension?
Authenticity?

"Why don't you climb it?" Harris said coolly, looking up at the top of the water tower.

"I am not afraid," Lacey answered. She was the only one in her gym class who had gone straight up the climbing rope without flinching, let go with one hand, and twirled around like a circus performer until the gym teacher made her climb down.

"I do not believe you will do it," Harris said.

"I will, actually."

"Go ahead then."

"All right."

Lacey shot up the ladder faster than Harris would have thought she could—faster than he could do it himself, he admitted, though he didn't say so aloud. She turned around to grin at him—and that's when it happened. The next to last rung, rusty from the weather, gave way, badly scratching Lacey's right foot.

"Ow," she said. "My foot is hurting."

"Wait there," Harris said. "It will be fine."

©2009. Allyn & Bacon, a division of Pearson Education. Developed by Vicki Spandel. All rights reserved.

Suggested Revisions of C and D

Sample C: Whole Class Revision

Every single day of his life, Paul wished his family lived in the city. His friends all thought it was so great living on a farm. Let them try it on chicken butchering day. That was enough to cure anyone of romantic notions about farm life, Paul figured.

"Let's go,
~~"Come on,~~ Paul," his dad said, grabbing some gloves and heading

"Putting this off won't make it any easier."
for the chicken pen. ~~"This is a hard task."~~

"It might,"   "It might make it go away altogether."
~~"Yes, it is,"~~ Paul answered.

"Very funny, Paul,"   shot back,
~~"It's a good thing I have you to help,"~~ his dad ~~added,~~ ignoring

Paul's lack of enthusiasm.

"Look, this isn't working for me. I'm thinking of turning vegetarian,"
~~"I would prefer not to participate,"~~ Paul replied—at which point

a bit skeptical.
his dad looked ~~very puzzled.~~

"Nice try,"
~~"It is not anyone's favorite task,"~~ he said. "But ~~butchering a~~

number one, you hate spinach and broccoli, and for another thing, if we
~~chicken will give us something good to eat,"~~ don't do this, we won't have
                                                                            any dinner."
"We could always fast—or
Paul shrugged. ~~"Perhaps we could~~ buy our chicken from the

like normal people,"   "At least those chickens aren't pets with names."
store, he suggested. ~~"Those chickens are not pets."~~

©2009. Allyn & Bacon, a division of Pearson Education. Developed by Vicki Spandel. All rights reserved.

Sample D: Revising with Partners

"Do it—I double dare ya,"
~~"Why don't you climb it?"~~ Harris said coolly, looking up at the top of the water tower.

"You think I won't? I'm not afraid of some stupid water tower!"
~~"I am not afraid."~~ Lacey answered. She was the only one in her gym class who had gone straight up the climbing rope without flinching, let go with one hand, and twirled around like a circus performer until the gym teacher made her climb down.

"I think you're scared. I think you're shaking," Harris taunted her.
~~"I do not believe you will do it," Harris said.~~ could climb a tower twice that high. You're the one who's scared."
~~"I will, actually."~~

"Stop talking about it then, acrobat, and do it."
~~"Go ahead then."~~

"Watch this, groundling."
~~"All right."~~

Lacey shot up the ladder faster than Harris would have thought she could—faster than he could do it himself, he admitted, though he didn't say so aloud. She turned around to grin at him—and that's when it happened. The next to last rung, rusty from the weather, gave way, badly scratching Lacey's right foot.

"Ow," she ~~said~~ screamed. "My foot is ~~hurting.~~ about to break off! I can't even stand on it!"

~~"Wait there,"~~ "Stop whining and hang on!" Harris said. ~~"It will be fine."~~ "The groundling is coming to rescue you."

©2009. Allyn & Bacon, a division of Pearson Education. Developed by Vicki Spandel. All rights reserved.

Editing Wrap-Up
(All Editing Lessons for Grade 6)

Trait Connection: **Conventions**

Introduction (Share with students in your own words.)

In this lesson, you will have a chance to practice editing for errors and problems covered in *all* 14 previous editing lessons. An editing checklist is provided to remind you what to look for.

Teaching the Lesson (General Guidelines for Teachers)

1. Begin by making copies of the editing checklist (page 247) and passing this out to students. Review anything that they do not recall. Encourage students to keep this list for future reference. You may wish to laminate it so students can mark it with a dry erase marker, or insert it into a plastic protective cover.

2. Review some basic copy editor's marks, such as the caret (∧), delete symbol (◯), circled dot for a period⊙ —and mark for a new paragraph: ¶

3. Review the procedure for inserting punctuation/text using a caret, or inserting quotation marks using an inverted caret: ∧ ᐁ ᐁ

4. Provide any lists that may be helpful: e.g., list of negatives, chart of confusing words. Give students access to a handbook, if you wish.

5. Share the editing lesson on the next page.

6. Students should read the passage aloud (*softly*), looking at *and listening* for errors or problems. They will encounter *at least one error* emphasized in each lesson. (*Note:* Use of ellipsis or dash is optional. Students should simply check to see that these marks are used correctly.)

7. Ask them to edit individually first, then check with a partner.

8. When everyone is done, ask them to coach you as you edit the same copy, making any changes you and they identify. Use carets, inverted carets, and delete symbols to make your corrections. Circle new periods.

9. When you finish, read your edited copy aloud to make sure you caught *everything*, pausing to discuss your editorial changes. Compare your version to our suggested copy on page 249.

10. If students have any difficulty, review as necessary and repeat this lesson, asking students to work with different partners.

Editing Goal: Correct 24 errors (including marking 5 new paragraphs).
Follow-Up: Look for editorial changes needed in your own work.

Editing Checklist

___ I used carets (^) to insert words or corrections.

___ I used the delete symbol (ᗧ) to take things out.

___ I used commas in a series: *We had liver, broccoli, and spaghetti for dinner.*

___ I used commas in compound sentences: *We thought it would rain, but we hadn't prepared for snow.*

___ I corrected run-on sentences (*Brenda fell she got right up again*) by (1) adding a conjunction, (2) inserting a semicolon, or (3) writing two sentences:

Brenda fell, **but** *she got right up again.*

Brenda fell; she got right up again.

Brenda fell. She got right up again.

___ I used a dash to show emphasis—just like this.

___ I used parentheses (another mark of punctuation) to add noncritical info.

___ I used ellipsis to . . . well . . . take a pause.

___ I put commas and periods that were part of the speech inside quotation marks:

"Be quiet," she said.

She said, "Be quiet right now."

___ I put question marks and exclamation points inside quotation marks if they were part of the speech—and outside if they were not:

She asked, "Which way is the remodeled observation tower?"

Did she call it the "remodeled observation tower"?

___ I started a new paragraph with every new speaker.

___ I used **lie** to mean *recline: He needed to* **lie** *down.*

___ I used **lay** to mean *set down:* **Lay** *the contract on my desk.*

___ I was careful with confusing words: *accept/except, all ready, already, all together/ altogether, principle/principal.*

___ I corrected all double negatives:

I **can't hardly** *see the sunset from here.*

Changed to—

I **can hardly** *see the sunset from here,* or

I **can't** *see the sunset from here.*

___ I read *everything* silently AND aloud, pencil in hand.

Editing Practice

Goal: Correct any errors. *Don't forget to mark new paragraphs!*

Maria, Carlos, and Andrea were working on a school project altogether.

They didn't hardly have enough time. They needed to choose a topic

conduct interviews and create a visual presentation— all by Friday. It

was all ready Tuesday. "This is not going to be easy" Maria said with a

sigh. "You're telling me, Carlos answered. He hated projects he always

seemed to have a hard time finishing. "Shall we divide up the work "

Andrea suggested Everyone thought that was an excellent idea—

especially with time running out. They all laid down on the carpet and

stared at the ceiling, so they could think better. They lay their notes in a

pile next to them. We're in this all together," Maria said. "Everyone

accept me, Carlos said—then added, "Just kidding! But Carlos was

right. There wasn't no way they could finish. Then, out of the blue . . . it

came to them—a project on doing projects! Beautiful! "There isn't

nothing we know more about! exclaimed Maria. It wasn't going to take

hardly any effort!

©2009. Allyn & Bacon, a division of Pearson Education. Developed by Vicki Spandel. All rights reserved.

Edited Copy

(24 errors corrected, 6 paragraphs total)

Maria, Carlos, and Andrea were working on a school project ~~altogether~~ **all together.**

They didn't ~~hardly~~ have enough time. They needed to choose a topic,

conduct interviews, and create a visual presentation—all by Friday. It

was ~~all ready~~ **already** Tuesday. "This is not going to be easy," Maria said with a

sigh. ¶ "You're telling me," Carlos answered. He hated projects, he

always seemed to have a hard time finishing. ¶ "Shall we divide up the

work?" Andrea suggested. Everyone thought that was an excellent

idea—especially with time running out. They all ~~laid~~ **lay** down on the carpet

and stared at the ceiling, so they could think better. They ~~lay~~ **laid** their notes

in a pile next to them. ¶ "We're in this all together," Maria said.

¶ "Everyone ~~accept~~ **except** me," Carlos said—then added, "Just kidding!" But

Carlos was right. There wasn't ~~no~~ **any** way they could finish. Then, out of

the blue . . . it came to them—a project on doing projects! Beautiful!

¶ "There isn't ~~nothing~~ **anything** we know more about!" exclaimed Maria. It ~~wasn't~~ **was hardly**

going to take ~~hardly~~ any effort!

©2009. Allyn & Bacon, a division of Pearson Education. Developed by Vicki Spandel. All rights reserved.

Edited Copy (as it would appear in print)

Maria, Carlos, and Andrea were working on a school project all together. They didn't have enough time. They needed to choose a topic, conduct interviews, and create a visual presentation—all by Friday. It was already Tuesday. "This is not going to be easy," Maria said with a sigh.

"You're telling me," Carlos answered. He hated projects; he always seemed to have a hard time finishing.

"Shall we divide up the work?" Andrea suggested. Everyone thought that was an excellent idea—especially with time running out. They all lay down on the carpet and stared at the ceiling, so they could think better. They laid their notes in a pile next to them.

"We're in this all together," Maria said.

"Everyone except me," Carlos said—then added, "Just kidding!" But Carlos was right. There wasn't any way they could finish. Then, out of the blue . . . it came to them—a project on doing projects! Beautiful!

"There isn't anything we know more about!" exclaimed Maria. It was hardly going to take any effort!

Note
We printed the first paragraph flush left. If you indented it, that is fine, and that would make 25 corrections in all.

©2009. Allyn & Bacon, a division of Pearson Education. Developed by Vicki Spandel. All rights reserved.

Notes

Notes

Notes

Notes

Notes

Notes

Notes

Notes